Britain's Scenic Railways:
The Waverley Route

Ashley Butlin and Iona Butlin

www.crecy.co.uk

© Ashley Butlin and Iona Butlin 2017

ISBN 9780711038523

First published 2017 by Crécy Publishing Ltd

A CIP record for this book is available from the British Library

Publisher's Note: Every effort has been made to identify and correctly attribute photographic credits. Any error that may have occurred is entirely unintentional.

Printed in Malta by Gutenberg Press

Crécy Publishing Limited
1a Ringway Trading Estate
Shadowmoss Road
Manchester M22 5LH

www.crecy.co.uk

Front Cover:
Class 158 No. 158741 heads south towards Stow on 10 September 2015. *Iona Butlin*

Rear Cover:
On 8 October 2015 the 'A4' *Union of South Africa* bursts under the bridge at Fushiebridge as it heads south climbing towards Borthwick Bank and Falahill. *Ashley Butlin*

Left:
The picturesque location of Canonbie station on 16 July 1962 as No 43139 waits to depart to Riddings Junction. *Bruce McCartney collection*

Middle:
A two-car DMU pauses at Rosewell & Hawthornden station with a train from Edinburgh to Peebles. The introduction of units on the line failed to halt the decline in traffic. *G. Norman Turnbull*

Right:
On 26 August 2016, Class 158 No 158782 departs for Edinburgh. *Iona Butlin*

Contents

Acknowledgements

This book would not have been possible without the help and advice of a number of people. I must thank my daughter Iona for the many hours we spent together traversing the Scottish Borders seeking out historic locations and artefacts in addition to the time we spent recording the rebuilding of the line. Some of the best times were tracking the various steam specials along the route. Thank you to my wife Jenny to whom I am always indebted for her patience, understanding, advice and proofreading although I must point out that any errors are mine and mine alone. Working on a project of this nature always brings new friendships, this being no exception. Bruce McCartney has helped enormously in steering me through the history of the Waverley Route: his knowledge being equal to his generosity with access to his large photographic collection which he made readily available. Similarly Norman Turnbull also allowed use of his colour photographs from the final years of the original Waverley Route. To Douglas Yuill I extend my thanks for helping identify the numerous Lothian pits associated with the history of the Edinburgh & Dalkeith Railway, and the later Waverley Route. Hamish Stevenson has equally helped with supplying older photographs.

Tom Pyemont was more than generous in allowing access to the restored Hassendean station site as also was Cook's Van hire, St Boswells, for letting us photograph the former St Boswells shed site. A number of landowners assisted with lineside access for photography – you know who you are and we thank you for your help.

To the various employees at Network Rail and ScotRail who readily allowed us access to various events we say 'thank you'. Similarly we thank the Network Rail Press Office for the regular press releases which have proved invaluable.

Bibliography

Border Country Branch Line Album, Neil Caplan, Ian Allan Publishing

Borders Railway Rambles, Alasdair Wham, Stenlake Publishing

Borders Railway: The Return Journey, Peter Ross, Lily Publications

Carlisle to Hawick, Roger Darsley & Dennis Lovett, Middleton Press

Galashiels to Edinburgh, Roger Darsley & Dennis Lovett, Middleton Press

Hawick to Galashiels, Roger Darsley & Dennis Lovett, Middleton Press

Last Years of The Waverley Route, David Cross, OPC

Memories of Lost Border Railways, Bruce McCartney, Self Published

Rails across the Border, Alexander Mullay, Tempus

Rail Centres: Carlisle, Peter W. Robinson, Booklaw Publications

Rail Centres: Edinburgh, A. J. Mullay, Booklaw Publications

The Railways of Peebles, Roy Perkins, Amberley

The Waverley Route, Ann Glen, Lily Publications

The Waverley Route, Neil Caplan, Ian Allan Publishing

The Waverley Route through Time, Roy Perkins, Amberley

Waverley: Portrait of a Famous Route, Roger Siviter, Runpast

Introduction

When Class 158 No 158701 departed from the new Tweedbank station for Edinburgh on 6 September 2015 it was the culmination of a vision of many who had long dreamed of the former Waverley Route once again echoing to the sound of trains running through picturesque valleys and climbing to Falahill, once a daunting prospect for steam-hauled services and still a challenge today where diesel multiple-units noticeably decrease their speed on the ascent to the summit. Scepticism that the line would never be built or be a complete white elephant were rapidly dispelled as passenger numbers soared beyond all expectations or predictions. When former LNER 'A4' Pacific No 60009 *Union of South Africa* was hired to run a number of steam specials during September and October 2015, interest in the re-opened line extended way beyond the nucleus of railway enthusiasts and commuters who quickly saw the potential of the new service, as tourists and local Border folk turned out in increasing numbers to watch and use the new line. Numbers hit an unprecedented level in 2016 when on 15 May 2016 arguably one of the most famous of all steam locomotives former LNER 'A3' No 60103 *Flying Scotsman* returned to the line hauling a charter service through to Tweedbank. Thousands lined the route, and traffic on the parallel A7 road was brought to a standstill near Bowland by inconsiderate motorists parking at random in the road to view the train! When official passenger numbers were released in 2016 for the first six months of services it was immediately clear that the decision to rebuild the line as far as Tweedbank was totally vindicated.

As to the future, at the time of writing there is considerable talk about extending the line further south, initially to Hawick. Whether a business case can be made to continue to Carlisle given the distance and almost total lack of population to be tapped remains to be seen. The potential for moving timber out of the vast Kielder Forest is a distinct possibility, given the number of lorry movements that could be taken off local roads, and it would be a definite draw linked with the existing timber facilities already present at Carlisle Kingmoor Yard.

Away from the towns such as Hawick, Galashiels and Melrose, the Scottish Borders remain remote and one of the most sparsely populated areas of the British Isles. One can drive for miles on back roads and meet very few other motorists, and see only isolated farms and cottages. In the summer, the valleys trap the heat, and the peace and quiet makes it idyllic for residents and visitors alike. The scenery, whilst lacking the grandeur of the Highlands, is spectacular and attracts walkers, cyclists, artists and wildlife enthusiasts to name but a few. However, in winter this remoteness brings its own problems. Main roads are usually treated and kept clear of snow and ice, but only limited numbers of side roads can be treated. Four-by-four vehicles are essential, as are good reserves of food for when conditions make shopping impossible. It doesn't take too much imagination to realise that this has been the norm for many years; only the development of metalled roads and motorised vehicles has changed travel over time.

Looking north from above Hawick towards the Eildon Hills.
Iona Butlin

The Waverley Route

At a time when travel in the Borders could only be undertaken on foot or by horse, the opening of the railway from Edinburgh to Hawick in 1849 caused a variety of reactions, from some landowners who were unhappy for their lands to be acquired for the construction to the mill owners in Galashiels and Hawick who found themselves with an efficient means of not only getting their goods away from the Borders to Edinburgh and beyond but also the means to bring in coal to enhance power to the mills previously totally dependent on water, so enabling existing businesses to expand, and new ones to open. Building large auction marts at St Boswells and Hawick also made it easier for farmers to move their livestock out of the area. For the general public, the opening of the railway brought about vast changes in their lives. In an area once totally self sufficient, now goods and produce could be brought into the area from anywhere in the country, from fresh produce not easily grown in the Borders to regional goods never previously seen.

Historically, many pictures of the Waverley Route were taken on the section south of Hawick where the line climbed up to Whitrope summit before heading south downhill towards Newcastleton. This stretch of the line ran through open barren moorland, remote and largely uninhabited. Since closure of the line in 1969, large tracts of this moorland has been planted with coniferous woodland, completely altering the views of the original route. Winter snowstorms caused frequent blockage of the line on this stretch, sometimes for quite considerable lengths of time. Whether this would still occur today should the line be reinstated through to Carlisle is difficult to tell or would the trees act as windbreaks and limit the encroachment of the snow across the lines?

The Waverley Route was one of those in Britain along with the Somerset & Dorset which gained a cult status. Following the Second World War, with steam still at its zenith, enthusiasts frequented the line to experience the delights of the variety of locomotives employed on the services. In addition the line provided numerous opportunities for photographers hence the plethora of scenic albums published over the years. Following the closure in 1969, interest in the line continued unabated including the failed Border Union Railway preservation attempt that sadly came to naught.

Following the re-opening of the northern end of the line between Newcraighall and Tweedbank in 2015 (two stations that didn't exist in 1969), interest has again been re-energised especially amongst a younger group of enthusiasts who never knew or travelled on the line in former days.

Many books have been written about the Waverley Route over the years and there are those who would perhaps question whether yet another title can add to previous volumes. It is to be hoped that a different approach to the subject will be achieved with this new publication which firstly looks at the history of the line from its inception in the 19th century during the height of railway mania, through to its closure by Dr Richard Beeching in 1969. Secondly it looks in detail at the rebuilding and re-opening of the line from Newcraighall (Edinburgh) and Tweedbank south of Galashiels in 2015. Finally it takes the reader on a photographic journey south of Tweedbank through Melrose, St Boswells and Hawick to show the features and structures still visible to enthusiasts before the next stages of re-opening hopefully take place.

The Waverley Route at closure in 1969.
By Pechristener – Own work, map was created using Open Street Map, CC BY-SA 2.0,
https://commons.wikimedia.org/w/index.php?curid=39303110

The Waverley Route
– Its Rise and Demise

During the 18th century, travel throughout the Borders was extremely difficult, and movement of commodities such as coal, limited. Southeast of Edinburgh lay the Lothian coalfields but getting the coal to Edinburgh, where there was an insatiable appetite for the fuel, was far from easy. Edinburgh was in the midst of major development as the New Town was being built. Demand for coal in the large new houses was immense. One only has to look at these houses today and see the array of chimney pots to appreciate the number of fireplaces requiring feeding. While canals brought coal to Edinburgh from the Lanarkshire fields west of the city, no such facility existed for the Lothian mines. As early as 1817 the mine owners looked at constructing a wagon-way to convey coal to the city. In the event, nothing came of this initial proposal. However, this was not the end of the project and in 1824 a further meeting of interested parties including the Duke of Buccleuch resulted in an Act of Parliament being passed on 26 May 1826 to allow for the construction of a line from St Leonards (south Edinburgh) to Dalhousie (South Esk). The line, Scotland's first railway, was built to the 'Scotch' gauge of 4ft 6in and was a horse-drawn wagon-way. In addition to building the line to Dalkeith and Dalhousie, a branch opened to Fisherrow, a harbour west of Musselburgh, followed in 1835 with a single-line branch to a terminus at Constitution Street, Leith, the port for Edinburgh.

The line from St Leonards opened on 4 July 1831 but only as far as a coal pit at Craighall. It was extended to Dalhousie Mains by October 1831. The Fisherrow branch opened on the same day. Along the route to Dalhousie, a considerable number of pit owners constructed their own links to the tramway in order to get their coal to the city. At the Dalhousie 'terminus' of the route, the line stopped at the north side of the River South Esk. Across the river lay the pits of the Marquis of Lothian at Arniston. To link to the tramway, the Marquis constructed a 1½ mile line from Dalhousie to the pits at Arniston.

Included in the extension was a bridge crossing the river at a length of 1,011 feet. Constructed at the expense of the Marquis, the line became known as 'The Marquis of Lothian Waggonway' and opened on 21 January 1832, allowing coal to be moved from Bryans pit. Later developments saw the Lingerwood Colliery linked to the line.

By 1838, the Edinburgh & Dalkeith Railway (E&DR) had constructed a short branch from the south end of the North Esk viaduct into Dalkeith. The line opened on 26 November 1838, initially for goods, but it is believed passengers were possibly also carried from the opening.

Like the Marquis of Lothian, the Duke of Buccleuch owned mines northeast of Dalkeith at Smeaton and Cowden so he also built lines at his own expense to join with the newly opened station at Dalkeith, with the line opening in 1839.

The E&DR was clearly a successful venture and soon after opening it was carrying 300 tonnes of coal each day to its goods yard at St Leonards. Soon after the E&DR had opened, on 2 June 1832, local businessman Michael Fox introduced a passenger service on the line between St Leonards and North Esk. Utilising a horse-drawn stagecoach, three return trips were made each day. In the first year of operation, an estimated 150,000 passenger journeys were recorded. Clearly buoyed by the success of Fox's venture, the E&DR obtained powers in 1834 to run its own passenger service and in 1836 took over Fox's operations.

Situated on the south side of the city close to Arthur's Seat, St Leonards was the location for Edinburgh's first railway station, opening to coal traffic in 1831. Passenger

The original Edinburgh & Dalkeith Railway.

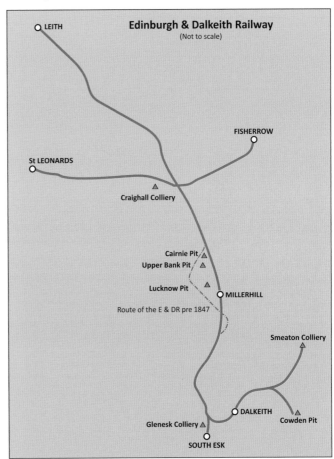

Above and left: The Edinburgh to Dalkeith Railway had its terminus at St Leonards in the shadow of Holyrood Park. Whilst it only lasted as a passenger station until 1847 when services were diverted to Waverley station, the site remained open for goods traffic until final closure in 1968. Today, surprisingly, one of the goods sheds remains although looking empty and out of use when viewed in the summer of 2016. Its railway origins are clear to see but its future is far from certain. *Iona Butlin (both)*

Below: On the approach to St Leonards, the Edinburgh to Dalkeith Railway ran through a tunnel built on a considerable gradient. Like so many former railway routes around Edinburgh, this has been converted to a cycle/walking route linking the east end to the city centre and was in constant use when viewed in August 2016. *Iona Butlin*

services followed in the summer of the following year. However, services only ran until 1847 when they were diverted to the newly opened North Bridge station which opened in June 1846, later being renamed Waverley in April 1866. From then until its closure in 1968, St Leonards was a goods depot, largely for the transfer of coal from rail to road.

Heading out of St Leonards, the E&DR was on a 1 in 30 gradient for the first two-thirds of a mile, including a 566-yard tunnel. This section was initially worked as a roped incline with two stationary engines.

Today little remains of the site with the exception of one of the goods sheds. Houses fill the majority of the site although the tunnel remains open, and like many former railway routes in Edinburgh has been converted to a footpath/cycleway.

Railway development in the 1840s reached fever pitch with numerous plans and proposals being put forward. Buoyed by the success of the E&DR, the company proposed extending to Hawick under the title of the Edinburgh & Hawick Railway. In the event, the E&DR was sold to the more prosperous and ambitious North British Railway (NBR) who purchased it for £113,000 in 1845.

When taken over by the NBR in 1845, the horse-drawn railway built to the Scotch gauge was converted to standard gauge of 4ft 8½in and became steam locomotive hauled, horse-drawn operations coming to a close.

At the time the NBR took over the E&DR in October 1845 a passenger station had existed at Portobello, on the line from St Leonards to Leith, since March 1835. It remained in use until 1846 when a second station was opened on 22 June 1846 on the nearby direct NBR line from Berwick to Edinburgh.

Further south, a station was opened at Niddrie on 4 July 1831. However, it was short lived and closed by October 1847, soon after the line was taken over by the NBR. A further short-lived station was located at Cairnie on the site of the present Millerhill Yard. Opened in October 1831 for goods and for passengers in 1832, it was closed in June 1846. Arguably more of a bus stop than a conventional railway station, Cairnie was a stopping on and off location on a minor road. The line at this point deviated from the later Waverley Route and moved nearer to Shawfair in order to service three small coal pits, namely Cairnie, Upper Bank and Lucknow.

The next station heading south was at Sheriffhall, the exact location being uncertain but either somewhere near where the A6106 Old Dalkeith Road crosses the railway by the junction with Melville Gate Road or possibly further north where the now City Bypass crosses the original route of the Waverley near Sheriffhall Mains. It opened on 2 June 1832 and was another to be closed in June 1846. As with other locations it is almost certain that this was not a station as we know them today but more of a 'bus stop' where the horse-drawn vehicles stopped to allow passengers on and off.

Glenesk station was located at the site of Glenesk Junction but was only in use for a few years. First appearing in Bradshaw in October 1855, it closed on 1 November 1874 although it remained as an unadvertised halt through to at least 1886. There were no freight facilities although a private siding north of the station served Glenesk Colliery.

Lasswade Road was yet another location surrounded by uncertainty not least that its exact location is not clear. Given its name it is assumed that it was located either north or south of Lasswade Road, Eskbank, possibly on the south side where Eskbank station was later located. It is thought to have opened in around 1842-43 and, similar to Cairnie, it may have been no more than a stopping point. When the railway was taken over by the North British and re-gauged to 4ft 8½in the location ceased to be used.

The final station at this time was located at South Esk just north of the Lothianbridge Viaduct and opened on 2 June 1831. When rebuilt to operate at the standard gauge of 4ft 8½in it re-opened on 21 June 1847, and was renamed Dalhousie on 12 July 1847.

The route following NBR takeover showing the extensions to Fushiebridge and colliery workings.

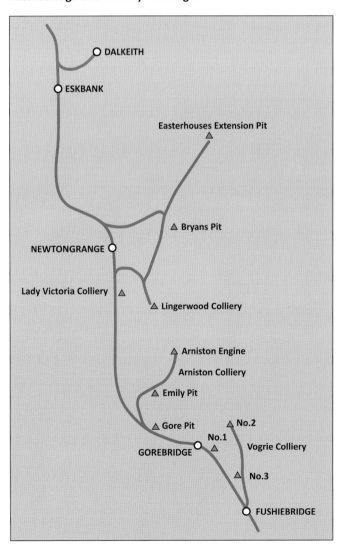

Following the NBR acquisition of the line, in addition to the closure of the stations previously mentioned, the company re-routed the line in the Millerhill area and opened a new station at Millerhill on 21 June 1847 near Easter Millerhill which was built to replace the stops at Cairnie and Sheriffhall. A second new station was opened at Gallowshill in July 1849. This was renamed Eskbank in 1850. Located between Lasswade Road and Bonnybrigg Road, the station was built in a cutting with an impressive station house which survives today as a private residence. An open lattice footbridge linked the ticket office at the top of the bank with the two platforms. No freight facilities were provided as the nearby Hardengreen Junction yard served the area. When work commenced to rebuild the line in 2012 the footbridge was removed and donated to the Waverley Route Heritage Association, Whitrope. In addition, this is one of the very few locations on the new Borders Railway where the original platforms remain in situ although the present Eskbank station is located several hundred yards further south near to the Midlothian campus of Edinburgh College.

In May 1845 a Parliamentary Committee considered the Bill for the Edinburgh & Hawick Railway. Amongst those speaking in favour of the line was no less than Isambard Kingdom Brunel, already well known for his work on the Great Western Railway. Although he had not visited Scotland, he assured the Committee that the proposed gradients and curvatures of the line, whilst being steep and tight, were no worse than those encountered on the Great Western Railway especially in Devon and Cornwall and well within the capabilities of locomotives of the era.

The very nature of the topography of the Southern Uplands dictated the route south initially to Galashiels. Falahill was the highest point on the route and involved a steep climb either side of the summit. On the north side, between Gorebridge and Falahill, an extensive embankment at Borthwick needed to be constructed. An initial proposal for a tunnel at Tynehead was rejected and a deep cutting constructed. In general this was the accepted policy, cuttings being less expensive to construct and maintain compared to tunnels. Consequently, between Edinburgh and Hawick only two tunnels were built, at Bowshank (249 yards) and the much shorter Torwoodlee tunnel (68 yards). Just north of the Torwoodlee tunnel, the line runs through the very deep Torwoodlee cutting, now bounded by the local golf course.

Located at the south end of Millerhill Yard on Old Craighall Road, the former Millerhill station opened on 21 June 1847 and remained open to passengers until it closed on 7 November 1955. South of the station a junction gave access to the Glencorse branch and later the now closed Bilston Glen colliery although the first part of the track remains along with an operational signal light! Today the station building has been extended and altered and is a private residence. *Iona Butlin*

The original Eskbank station was situated in a cutting north of the present station which has been built in a more convenient location to serve 21st century requirements. *Bruce McCartney collection*

At Bowshank Hill, the Gala Water took a large bow round the hill, the A7 following the same route, whilst the railway tunnelled through, the only significant tunnel between Edinburgh and Hawick. Major roads were crossed by overbridges but level crossings were employed on a number of minor roads where road and rail were on the level such as at Heriot and Fountainhall. Further south at Bowland, although a level crossing was proposed, in the event the road was lowered to provide an underpass to allow school children to cross the line safely. South of Falahill, the line crossed the Gala Water at numerous locations, and a variety of bridges were constructed, many of which were retained and refurbished for the re-opening of the line in 2015, a tribute to their original construction.

With the necessary Parliamentary Bill in place, the NBR continued south constructing the line towards Hawick from Dalhousie.

South of the Lothianbridge Viaduct, the line followed a circuitous route through to Newtongrange. This was one of the last stations to open, on 1 August 1908, following expansion of collieries in the area with associated housing. It replaced Dalhousie station 1½ miles to the north which closed on the same day. Located in a cutting, the station consisted of two platforms linked by a footbridge. The ticket office was located on Station Road above the cutting with steps leading down to the platform or across the footbridge. The station was downgraded to the status of an unstaffed halt on 5 December 1960. As with other stations, it was closed on 6 January 1969.

The magnificence of Lothianbridge Viaduct is clearly shown in this photograph taken in the 1960s. Today, trees and vegetation make this view of the viaduct impossible to recreate.
I. Holoran, Bruce McCartney Collection

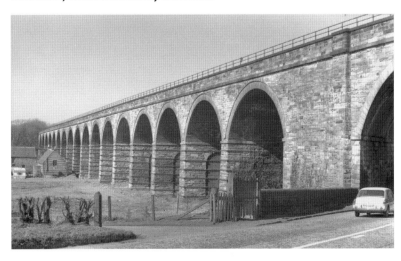

The next station was Gorebridge. Here, the station was built on a curve, with the two platforms staggered. When first opened on 14 July 1847 Gorebridge was named Gore Bridge, being renamed Gorebridge in 1872. From Gorebridge the line continued its increasing climb towards Falahill which it reached via Borthwick Bank. Observers of the line today cannot but marvel at the building of the line through the difficult terrain by the gangs of navvies employed. Thousands of tonnes of soil and rock had to be moved to create an acceptable gradient within the limits of the line.

Gorebridge was associated with the manufacture of gunpowder and, when first built, the railway ran through two short tunnels south of the station presumably to protect the nearby gunpowder factories. These were later opened up to form cuttings. Within sight of the overbridge at the south end of Gorebridge station lies the hamlet of Fushiebridge. Built in a shallow cutting, the station here served only a small isolated community which later developed around the station. Yet another station to see its name changed, it was initially called Fushie Bridge when opened in about September 1847; it was renamed Fushiebridge in 1877. Three miles south of Fushiebridge, the line entered a deep cutting and the location of Tynehead station. Initial plans indicated the construction of a tunnel at this point but this was changed to a deep cutting, presumably because of construction and maintenance costs involving a tunnel. A ticket office and station house were built at the top of the cutting with steep footpaths leading down to the two platforms. These could still be identified in 2011 prior to construction of the new Borders Railway. A small goods yard on the same level as the ticket office was accessed from the up line south of the station. The site of the yard remains clearly visible while the station house and ticket office survive as a private residence.

Initially named Tyne Head, the station opened on 4 August 1848, being renamed Tynehead in March 1874. Once over the summit at Falahill the line dropped down approximately two miles to Heriot. Another small community, it was served by a station also opened on 4 August 1848, with staggered platforms either side of a level crossing connecting the community to the Edinburgh road (A7). A small goods yard was also provided on the up side north of the level crossing.

A further three miles south of Heriot lay Fountainhall which also opened on 4 August 1848. Initially it was named Burn House, but was quickly renamed Fountainhall in March 1849.

The line continued a downward meander following the Gala Water to Stow, approximately four miles from Fountainhall. Compared to the likes of the four previous stations, Stow served a more significant community, being around 150 inhabitants in 1848, with a small goods yard to the east of the station. The station here opened on 4 November 1848.

An interesting view of the cutting south of Tynehead station in April 1964 as 'B1' 4-6-0 No 61349 heads south and climbs towards the Borthwick Bank. The line in the background leads to the small goods yard behind the station booking office. Looking at the picture it would appear that the line to the goods yard is on an incline. In fact, it is the main line that is climbing while the siding is on the level – shades of the Electric Brae in Ayrshire! While the track has long gone, the route to the former is still clearly visible from passing trains on today's Borders Railway.
Robin Barbour, Bruce McCartney collection

At a time when DMUs were being repainted from green to blue, mixed liveries were not uncommon. Such a unit climbs the final few yards to Falahill summit and is about to pass under the A7 road which crossed the line at this point by means of a bridge. Ironically, although the bridge was removed following closure of the line, a new bridge was built for the re-opened railway. *G. Norman Turnbull*

Lying about 3½ miles further south, beyond Bowshank Tunnel, the next station was Bowland, also opened on 4 August 1848. This was another very rural location but included a small goods yard north of the station on the up side. For a time between May 1849 and July 1862 the station was renamed Bowland Bridge. Possibly due to its rural location, the station was closed in December 1953, 15 years before the axe fell on the rest of the line.

Emerging from the north end of Bowshank Tunnel, an unidentified 'Peak' heads an Anglo-Scottish express bound for Edinburgh. *G. Norman Turnbull*

Based on Haymarket depot, the BRWC Class 26s were a common sight on the Waverley Route during the final years of the line. No D5302 draws into the original Galashiels station with a train from Edinburgh bound for Carlisle. The new Galashiels station is located beyond the impressive signal box. *Robin Barbour, Bruce McCartney collection*

Beyond Bowland the route again went through a very deep cutting at Torwoodlee followed by the short Torwoodlee tunnel as the line approached Galashiels which the railway reached in 1849, the station opening on 20 February 1849.

Galashiels was the first significant centre of population the line encountered since leaving Edinburgh. Prior to the arrival of the railway, a journey by horse and cart took six hours on rough turnpike roads following the present route of the A7. On completion of the line, this journey time was greatly reduced both in time and cost. In addition it opened up the potential for the many mills associated with the town which had been responsible for its growth during the early 19th century. Galashiels was provided with a significant goods yard and a small engine shed. A new two-road shed was built in about 1903.

While the new Borders Railway serves Galashiels, the new station is located north of the site of the original station, with the vast majority of the original site now occupied by a supermarket. Interestingly, while all evidence of the former station has been cleared, the original ornate sandstone gateposts leading to the station still remain in place.

Following the climbs to Falahill, the route from Galashiels to Hawick was relatively level. Here the land is more fertile, and sheep farming gives way to arable crops. South of Galashiels the railway crossed the River Tweed by the

Redbridge Viaduct. Today the line enters Tweedbank station serving the newly developed community that not so many years ago was open countryside and Tweedbank was a mere farm. Four miles beyond Galashiels was Melrose. A substantial station building was provided here to serve this historic Border town.

Nestling below the Eildon Hills, Melrose station opened in February 1849 and was accompanied by a number of sidings on the downside behind the platform buildings. Road access to the goods yard was via a steep slope from the road passing under the line.

The up platform and station buildings remain today in use as a children's nursery. However, the downside platforms and buildings along with the goods yard located beyond this platform were all cleared to make way for the Melrose bypass.

Passing again into rural countryside, just over a mile from Melrose, a station was opened at Newstead in November 1849 along with small freight facilities. However, this was another station only opened for a very short time as in just under three years it closed in October 1852.

Turning south, the line continued a few miles to St Boswells, one of the more important locations on the route with branch lines north and south of the station. The station was set at road level with an impressive entrance leading up a flight of steps to platform level. An extensive set of sidings

Galashiels viewed in March 1969 following the closure of the line and it is obvious the amount of land taken up by the railway. The large Roman Catholic church in the background remains today while virtually everything else has been swept away. Even the iron girder bridge over the station was rebuilt prior to the re-opening of the line. Today, Asda's supermarket with its associated car park stands on the site of the engine shed along with much of the yard. The new line follows a narrow corridor to the right of the picture and rejoins the original route in Currie Road behind the photographer. *I. Holoran, Bruce McCartney Collection*

Located between Galashiels and St Boswells, Melrose remains a popular Borders town. It was thus in the mid 1800s when the railway arrived at the town. Looking south, the station was elevated above the town to the left. A small goods yard was located on the down side behind the platform. *G. Norman Turnbull*

Looking south at St Boswells with the engine shed to the left of the bay platform which was for the Kelso branch passenger trains. *Bruce McCartney collection*

accompanied the station built to the north and south especially to serve the two auction marts in the town. In addition, a small single-road shed built in 1849 to the north of the station was quickly replaced by a more substantial two-road shed in January 1863, and remains extant today.

Opened on 20 February 1849 the station was initially named Newtown Junction, being renamed Newtown St Boswells in January 1863, and St Boswells in March 1865, even though the location was in present day Newtown St Boswells, a short distance from the village of St Boswells!

During the Second World War an armaments factory was constructed in open fields near Charlesfield, south of Newtown St Boswells, for the production of incendiary bombs, producing around one million each month. Approximately 1,300 people were employed at the factory and, to bring them in from the surrounding towns, a halt was built on the overbridge with steep access steps constructed up from the road to the platforms. Opened on 10 August 1942, it closed by June 1961.

With the line now heading south, the extremely small hamlet of Belses approximately five miles from St Boswells followed. Interestingly, the station nameboard read 'For ANCRUM and LILLIESLEAF', 2½ and 3½ miles away respectively, indicative of the view held that walking that distance in rural Victorian days was quite acceptable given the advantages gained. A fascinating insight into the running of Belses station in NBR days was covered in an article in *Backtrack Magazine* Vol 8 No 1 Jan/Feb 1994. The style of the Belses station building was very similar to those built for the North British Railway on the Edinburgh Suburban Lines.

In addition, the footbridge looked almost too frail but it survived through to the end!

As the line approached Hawick, a further station was constructed at Hassendean four miles north of Hawick. Opened in 1850, this was yet another station equipped with a small goods yard ideally suited for the rural area with coal facilities and a cattle dock.

Hawick, the destination of the Edinburgh & Hawick Railway, was reached in 1849 and opened to the public on 29 October 1849. Situated on the north bank of the River Teviot alongside the now A7 road, the station was built as a terminus and was equipped with an extensive goods yard and an engine shed.

Having reached Hawick by the autumn of 1849 the NBR sought to extend the line south to Carlisle in an attempt to penetrate an area dominated by the Caledonian Railway (CR) – competition between the two major Scottish companies being particularly volatile. In fact the Caledonian Railway put forward its own proposal for a line from Carlisle to Hawick via Langholm, a route that, should it have reached fruition, would actually have been easier than the ultimate North British Railway route via Liddesdale and Newcastleton.

The lack of population south of Hawick was always going to be a vital consideration for any railway between Hawick and Carlisle, but the North British Railway was determined to prevent the CR penetrating into its area of operation, namely the Scottish Borders. Consequently it put forward plans for the Border Union Railway (BUR), the line receiving Royal Assent in July 1859. Work began within two months amid celebrations and much hype at Hawick.

Looking down on Hawick station and shed. Note the tall signal box which gave a clear view over the footbridge to the platforms beyond, and the southern approach to the station. *Bruce McCartney collection*

Former LNER Class A3 No 60068 *Sir Visto* allocated to Carlisle Canal shed enters Hawick station at the head of 'The Waverley', a north-bound service from London St Pancras, in the summer of 1958. The embankment at this point has been totally removed and is now Mart Street, a key link road in Hawick. *Robin Barbour, Bruce McCartney collection*

The 50-mile route from Hawick to Carlisle followed a circuitous and difficult terrain, not least including a steep climb to Whitrope Summit at 1,006ft, and one of the longest tunnels in Scotland on the approach to the summit from the north. Building of the line took three years and was split between nine contracts. Given the difficult terrain and the extreme weather conditions experienced, it is quite amazing that the line was built in the time scale.

Opening of the line commenced in stages, with Canal Junction to Scotsdyke taking place on 29 October 1861; to Newcastleton on 2 June 1862 and to Hawick on 1 July 1862. Given the domination of the CR north of Carlisle, and its antagonism of the NBR, the latter was faced with extreme difficulties in accessing Carlisle Citadel station. To overcome the problem the NBR acquired running rights over the Port Carlisle Railway & Dock Co. which it accessed at Canal Junction.

Continuing the journey south from Hawick, the railway was faced with crossing the River Teviot as the line headed south through the town. The first Hawick station was built as a terminus abutting the main Hawick to Edinburgh road (now the A7) at present day Dovemount Place. To take the line south, it swung through an almost 90-degree curve taking it high above the river. The new station was constructed on the curve with the platforms extending across the river, giving rise to the numerous photographs of this iconic location. Following the opening of the new station on 1 July 1862, the first station was incorporated into the goods depot.

Leaving Hawick the line passed to the east through the Lynwood area of the town where it crossed the Slitrig Water on a high viaduct and headed south. The first location was Stobs Camp, a private facility built to serve the large army camp opened in 1903. Consisting of a number of sidings capable of holding in the region of four troop trains, the station was reportedly linked to the camp by a horse-drawn narrow gauge tramway. Initially during the First World War the camp housed interned civilians prior to them being sent to the Isle of Man but soon became a Prisoner of War camp. It was again used for troop training during the Second World War and after the war became a resettlement centre for Polish Troops. It was used by the Territorial Army during the summer months of the 1950s before being closed towards the end of the decade. The station is believed to have closed in about 1959.

A little further on, four miles south of Hawick, was Stobs station. Initially named Barnes, the station was renamed Stobs within months of opening. A single siding to the northwest of the station was provided for local goods traffic.

Continuing the climb towards Whitrope Summit, the station at Shankend was a further three miles into the hills and just south of the very impressive Shankend Viaduct. With 15 arches, Shankend was, and still is, a most impressive structure constructed using greywacke rock. Even today, Shankend is in a wild and remote setting. The station was provided with three loop lines along with sidings for banking engines. Shankend station opened on 1 July 1862.

The Teviot Viaduct carried the railway (and platforms) across the River Teviot when the railway was extended to Carlisle. It was demolished in September 1975. *I. Holoran, Bruce McCartney Collection*

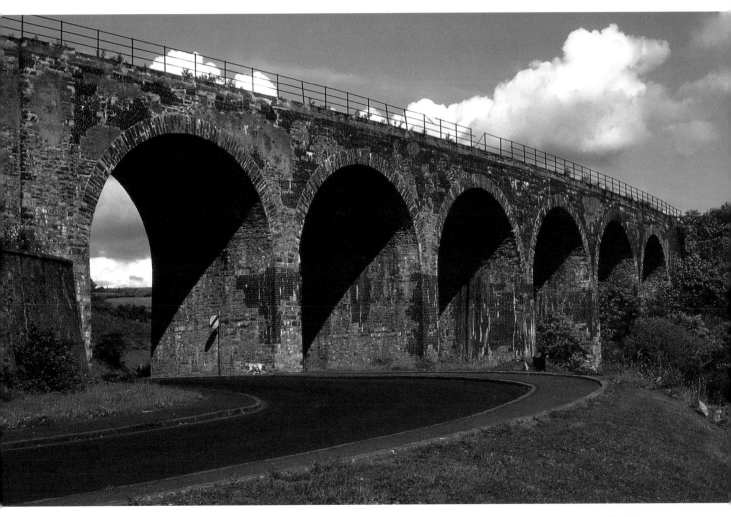

The impressive Slitrig Viaduct to the south of Hawick was demolished in 1982 following the closure reportedly due to children throwing ballast off the bridge onto cars travelling on the road below. Interestingly this bridge was also known as the Lynnwood Viaduct or locally as Six-Arch Brig. *G. Norman Turnbull*

Shankend Viaduct in all its splendour with an unidentified freight train climbing towards the summit at Whitrope. *Robin Barbour, Bruce McCartney collection*

One can almost feel the cold as a 'Britannia' Pacific No 70035 passes a snowy Whitrope Summit in November 1964 with the 8.16am Millerhill–Carlisle freight. Heavy snow in these wild parts of the Southern Uplands was a real problem during the winter months, blocked lines being a constant worry requiring engines on snow plough duty on stand-by when snow was forecast. *Robin Barbour, Bruce McCartney collection*

Climbing to the summit, the line passed through the 1,208-yard Whitrope Tunnel on a rising gradient of 1 in 90. Constructing the tunnel was far from easy and progress was slow and dangerous. Water ingress was huge and required remedial drainage works. Climbing out of the tunnel the line almost immediately crossed the summit prior to the 10-mile descent to Newcastleton. Whitrope Summit is today the home to the Waverley Route Heritage Association and its growing collection of rolling stock and artefacts.

Approximately two miles from Whitrope Summit, the line met with the Border Counties Railway at Riccarton Junction – one of the most unusual but well known railway locations in the country. Situated in the middle of nowhere, the junction was totally dependent on the railway as it held no road connections. Initially named just Riccarton, the 'Junction' was only added to the name on 1 January 1905. The location was supplied with numerous sidings and a three-lane locomotive shed. The location was the junction with the Border Counties Railway which came north from Northumberland. A considerable community developed at the location including 37 houses and a school. A branch of the Hawick Co-op and a post office operated out of the station buildings. The location was abandoned following closure of the line and today little remains to indicate the life that existed here for just over 100 years.

A wonderful view of the remote Riccarton Junction showing the extensive sidings and engine shed. The village lay to the left of the photograph. This legendary location, the junction with the Waverley Route and the Border Counties Railway, was remarkable for having no road connection – the only way in or out was by rail or on foot! *Bruce McCartney collection*

Newcastleton was one of just two stations of any significance between Hawick and Carlisle. Viewed looking north after the line closed, the goods yard lay to the right of the line. Note the track on the up side had started to be lifted.
G. Norman Turnbull

Approximately half-way on the descent from Whitrope Summit to Newcastleton was yet another remote station, serving isolated farms, namely Steele Road. Amongst the moorland hills, the opening of the station on 2 June 1862 must have totally changed the lives of the local population, putting Hawick just 45 minutes away, an amazing improvement on the days when they had to rely on horse power.

Five miles south of Steele Road lies Newcastleton; no more than a large village, it was the largest centre of population between Hawick and Longtown. The station opened on 1 March 1862 and was equipped with a number of sidings forming a small goods yard to the north of the station. The proximity of the Border forests allowed timber to be taken out by rail, thus keeping numerous lorries off the narrow roads in the area. In recent years the idea of removing timber from Kielder Forest has been much discussed, and could yet be a deciding factor when considering the re-opening of the line through to Carlisle.

South of Newcastleton the line crossed the border from Scotland into England prior to the railway reaching Kershopefoot, another small rural location, the station also opening on 1 March 1862. As with most stations it was equipped with limited goods facilities.

From Newcastleton through Kershopefoot and on to Penton, a total distance of just over seven miles, the route was relatively level compared with the steep climbs either side of Whitrope summit.

It is hard to believe today that 'private' stations were not uncommon back in the 19th century. Nook Pasture was one such location where just one train per week, the 7.47 am from Kershopefoot, stopped for the benefit of John Foster, a major shareholder of the NBR who lived at Nook. No buildings or goods facilities were provided and the station had closed by the end of 1873.

Penton was another station nowhere near a village or town and was named after Penton House. Interestingly, the station was equipped with a small goods yard to the north of the line.

With the route of the Border Union Railway bypassing Langholm, the NBR agreed to build a branch line to the town from Riddings Junction. Situated just over two miles south of Penton, the junction was another to open on 1 March 1862 although the branch itself didn't open until two years later. The station had three platform faces so as to allow the branch train not to impede the main lines. The location also had a goods yard north of the station. Little population surrounded Riddings but passenger numbers were good due to the interchange with the branch to Langholm.

Two miles further south the line came close to the now A7 road and a further rural station was built at Scotch Dyke. Initially named Scotsdyke when opened on 29 October 1861, it was later renamed Scotch Dyke in 1904. Once again the station served only a limited population, but the small goods yard generated mainly agricultural traffic. This was one of the earlier stations to close, on 2 May 1949. Perhaps surprisingly, the station building and associated cottages remain extant.

Former LMS 'Black Five' No 45481 hauls a mixed freight north through Riddings Junction. *Robin Barbour, Bruce McCartney collection*

Scotch Dyke station viewed some time after track lifting. The building remains in private use and has recently undergone considerable refurbishment. *Bruce McCartney collection*

'J39' 0-6-0 No 64895 from Carlisle Canal shed drifts into Longtown with a local service from Langholm on 28 July 1962.
Bruce McCartney collection

Longtown was one of the larger centres of population served by the BUR. The station was built to the west of the River Esk on the opposite side to the town. Facilities at Longtown included a goods yard and two-road engine shed, the latter reported closed in the 1920s. South of Longtown the Gretna Branch diverged to the west, while the main line crossed the River Esk on a viaduct, continuing south across open countryside.

Three miles on was Lyneside station. Opened on 29 October 1861 as West Linton, the nearest hamlet, it was renamed Lineside on 10 June 1870 and Lyneside in December 1871. As in most cases, the station had a small goods yard serving local needs. Although the station building was quite impressive, patronage of the station was low and it closed to passengers on 1 November 1929. Closure of the goods yard followed on 5 October 1964, while the station building remains today as a private residence.

A station opened at Harker on 29 October 1861, very much in line with all the other minor locations. Although less than five miles from Carlisle, Harker was still very much a rural location. Another early casualty, the station closed on 1 November 1929. However, this was not the end for the station as following the opening of Carlisle Airport on 23 March 1933, it re-opened in 1936. In 1939 the airport was taken over by the RAF with Harker station remaining open until it closed for a second time in October 1941 when the RAF moved to a new location at Crosby-on-Eden earlier in the year. The chequered history of Harker station continued when it was further re-opened on 1 March 1943, being located on the south side of the road overbridge. This station remained open until the closure of the line in 1969. Goods facilities

Lyneside is another former station that has found new life as a beautiful private residence. While today the location feels close to the expanding Carlisle, way back this was another remote station and closed in 1929. *Iona Butlin*

The station at Harker had a chequered career as it was opened and closed on a number of occasions. Once remote, as Carlisle has expanded over the years it is now on the edge of industrial units. Finally closed in 1969, the station building remains as a private residence. *Iona Butlin*

ceased on 27 December 1965. In connection with the development of RAF facilities to the north of Carlisle, a further station was opened specifically for military staff at Parkhouse Halt, south of Harker, on 7 July 1941. Officially the halt wasn't open to the general public but remained open until the closure of the line in 1969.

Approaching Carlisle, the Waverley Route passed over the Caledonian main line north of Kingmoor locomotive sheds and joined the route of the Port Carlisle Railway at Canal Junction. A small station was opened named Port Carlisle Junction on 29 October 1861 but had closed by 1 July 1864. The platform is still in existence in the Engine Lonning Nature Reserve.

From here the line ran through to Citadel station (designed by William Tate and opened on 4 September 1847), and to the NBR in 1861 when services commenced between Carlisle and Edinburgh on completion of the Waverley Route.

Branch Lines

No account of the Waverley Route would be complete without reference to the various branch lines feeding into the line. For those interested in lost lines, these branch lines contain considerable evidence of their past life from station buildings to bridges, and can reveal much for those taking the time to explore.

Dalkeith Branch

When the line from Edinburgh first opened, Dalkeith was the original terminus with the station opening in the autumn of 1839. Initially built to the Scotch Gauge of 4ft 6in, it was converted to standard gauge when re-opened in July 1847. The extension of the main line south towards Hawick resulted in the construction of a junction at Glenesk leaving the original line to Dalkeith as a branch. When built, Dalkeith was equipped with a single platform, and a goods yard.

Above: **Dalkeith was the terminus for the original Edinburgh & Dalkeith Railway. It opened as a passenger station in 1839, closing on 9 January 1942 but remaining open to goods until August 1964. In this view taken on 17 April 1955 the station platform is to the right. Today the site has been taken over by a supermarket. However, the two churches remain.** *Hamish Stevenson collection*

Beyond the station the line extended as the Dalkeith Colliery Railway to serve the local pits. This line remained in use until 1870 when the site at Dalkeith was rebuilt and extended with the colliery lines diverted to make a new connection with the Waverley Route at Hardengreen. Extending the facilities at Dalkeith in 1870 saw the goods yard enlarged, and a single road engine shed constructed. The engine shed closed in 1915. Passenger services ceased on 5 January 1942, while goods traffic continued until 8 August 1956.

Peebles Loop

As railway mania gripped the Scottish Borders, towns like Galashiels, Melrose and Hawick all flourished as opportunities for trade increased, not least with Edinburgh. Peebles, a small market town lies to the west of the NBR Waverley Route, but east of the Caledonian line from Carlisle to Glasgow and had lost out on the initial building of these two routes.

As early as 1810 Thomas Telford proposed a horse-drawn waggonway from Glasgow to Berwick-upon-Tweed passing through Peebles. A further scheme was proposed by Robert Stephenson in 1821 but nothing came of either schemes. A more serious idea in 1841 was that of the National Railway of Scotland for a line from Lancaster to Peebles where the line would divide with one branch going to Glasgow, the other to Edinburgh. This was yet another scheme that didn't get off the ground. When the Edinburgh & Hawick Bill was prepared it included a branch from Hawick north to Peebles but this was dropped before the Bill went before Parliament. Equally the Caledonian Railway also proposed a line to Peebles from their Glasgow route, this too being abandoned. Not to be outdone, a further group raised sufficient capital for a Bill to be put before parliament for a double-track line from Edinburgh to Peebles via Penicuik, but again, this fell by the wayside.

Finally, in 1851, three men from Peebles, William Chambers, Walter Thorburn and John Bathgate, proposed a line from Eskbank to Peebles via Bonnyrigg and Hawthornden. They called on well known railway man Thomas Bouch to survey the route and put forward a proposal for a line to be built as cheaply as possible! Consequently the 18¾-mile line was built with a capital of £70,000 with an additional borrowing available of £23,000.

In a ceremony at Peebles on 9 August 1853, the first sod was cut and construction commenced at both ends of the line by contractors Bray and Dyson. By March 1855 the contractors stated that the line would be complete and ready to open in May. The company owning the line purchased their own locomotives and rolling stock, and the locomotive *Soho* made the first trip from Peebles to Eskbank in the April. Passenger services commenced at the end of May when a special, with invited guests, arrived at Peebles on 29 May 1855.

The Peebles Railway remained independent until 1861 when it was absorbed into the NBR at a price of £20,000 which included all the rolling stock and locomotives. Prior to the takeover, the Peebles Railway ran three trains each day

between Peebles and Edinburgh, the coaches being conveyed between Eskbank and Edinburgh by the NBR.

Rivalry between the NBR and the CR raised its head again at this time. A further independent company, the Symington, Biggar & Broughton Railway (SB&BR), constructed a line off the Caledonian Railway main line from Glasgow to Carlisle in 1858, the line opening to Broughton on 5 November 1860. Earlier in the year, the company was granted parliamentary rights to extend the line to Peebles. Seeing this as a threat, the NBR gained the rights to extend its line from Peebles through to Galashiels. Three days later the SB&BR was taken over by the CR who possibly saw this as a way of getting a foothold into the Borders by building its own line from Peebles to Galashiels. In fact, by being pre-empted by the NBR, this plan never transpired and rivalry between the two companies over the battle for the Borders came to an end.

The line to Peebles from the north diverted from the NBR Waverley Route at Hardengreen Junction, travelling west to the first station at Bonnyrigg which opened a month after the rest of the line. Next was Rosewell & Hawthornden which opened at the same time as the rest of the line on 4 July 1855. Until 9 July 1928 the station was known simply as Hawthornden. Further west the line arrived at Rosslynlee. This was yet another station that carried a variety of names! Opening on 4 July 1855 it was called Roslin, becoming Rosslyn in 1864, and finally Rosslynlee in 1872.

Just beyond Rosslynlee station was Rosslynlee hospital. This had its own sidings where coal was delivered for the hospital boilers. Surprisingly, as late as 1958 a simple halt

A two-car DMU pauses at Rosewell & Hawthornden station with a train from Edinburgh to Peebles. The introduction of units on the line failed to halt the decline in traffic. *G. Norman Turnbull*

Peebles station and a DMU from Edinburgh to Galashiels waits on its route south. Today the A703 Edinburgh Road runs along this very location. *G. Norman Turnbull*

was opened to serve the hospital. With a platform length of only 22 yards and only open for four years, this was one of the shortest lived and smallest stations in Scotland.

Although later served by a direct branch line from Hawthornden Junction in 1872, Penicuik had a further station, albeit ½ mile away at Pomathorn. Initially it was called Penicuik until the Penicuik branch opened when it was renamed Pomathorn.

Beyond Pomathorn the line reached the highest point of the route at Leadburn where a station was built in an isolated location. In 1864 the Leadburn, Linton & Dolphinton Railway opened, resulting in Leadburn taking on a more prominent role.

Another private 'station', Earlyvale Gate was a request stop provided for less than a year from June 1856 to February 1857 for members of the Dundas family. The exact location is not clear but is thought to be near where a private road crossed the line near Earlyvale House.

From Leadburn the railway headed downhill south towards Peebles with a station at Eddleston, four miles from its destination. This was the first station to be located within the village itself. Initially built with a single platform, a loop and second platform was added later, providing a much needed passing place. The first station at Peebles was located in March Street and consisted of a single platform and station building. A small goods yard and engine shed were also provided.

It was on 1 October 1864 that the line to Galashiels opened as far as Innerleithen and through to Galashiels two years later on 18 June 1866. In order to extend the line, the original station in March Street was closed, becoming a goods yard, and the line extended south with a single platform station along with a new goods yard. In addition, connection was made with the Caledonian station to allow stock transfer between the two companies and very occasional special trains.

Leaving Peebles in an easterly direction, the line followed the route of the Innerleithen Road through to Cardrona. Today Cardrona is a large housing development but back in the 1850s it was just a small community only warranting a small station.

Innerleithen was the largest town between Peebles and Galashiels, and home to a number of mills. Accordingly, the station was equipped with a goods yard consisting of several sidings, a goods depot and cattle pens. Initially, Innerleithen was a temporary terminus until the line opened to Galashiels on 18 June 1866. Just a mile from Innerleithen is Walkerburn. For whatever reason, the station was not ready for the opening to Galashiels in June 1866 and didn't open until 15 January 1867. The station was supplied with the obligatory goods yard which included a goods shed. As the line continued east, the next station was Thornielee. Equipped with a small goods yard, patronage was never high and the station closed in November 1950.

Synonymous with rural lines in Victorian times was the provision of small private halts. Such a location existed for the Edinburgh Angling Club who owned a cottage called The Nest, and the halt named Angling Club Cottage Platform. It opened in 1898, closing after the Second World War.

The final station before Galashiels was at Clovenfords. Here a small goods yard was added by the end of the century. The arrival of the railway at Clovenfords allowed for the opening of the Tweed Vineyards in 1869, an enterprise that prospered for 90 years. Essential for the business was the need for many tonnes of coke delivered by rail required to heat hothouses.

The line joined the main Waverley Route north of Galashiels at Kilknowe Junction.

Peebles Loop

Whilst the Peebles loop was not directly part of the original Waverley Route, it has been included as trains using the loop started and ended on the Waverley via Hardengreen Junction, Dalkeith and Kilnknowe Junction, Galashiels. Interestingly, whilst it is unlikely trains will ever return to this picturesque route, a considerable number of artefacts remain, not least the majority of station buildings that have become private dwellings, along with bridges and the trackbed converted to walking/cycling routes. It is a line that can be visited for a day by car, or explored over a number of days on foot. The following is a small selection of photographs to whet the appetite of those wishing to explore the line.

Peebles was the original destination of the line and a good centre to start exploring the route. Very little remains of the railway and development has reclaimed the vast amount of former railway land to the point that the average visitor would have no idea that the town once boasted two stations, the Caledonian station with its line from Symington, and the station on the North British line. It is the latter that is the subject of this book. The first station of the Peebles Railway opened at March Street on 4 July 1855, the site today being partially occupied by a modern Tesco supermarket. When the line was extended to Galashiels this station was bypassed but remained active as a goods yard. A new station was built at the end of present day Dean Park Road on what is today the A703 Edinburgh Road. A plaque and mural at the side of the road (shown here) marks the site of the station.

Below: **This view looking north on the A703 shows the location in October 2016 of the station that opened in October 1864 and closed in February 1962, and can be roughly equated with the picture of the station on page 27.** *Iona Butlin*

Just off the A703 by a car park is the former goods yard weighbridge house, an innocuous building that has survived the changes of the past 60 years. Also near the A703/A72 roundabout is 'The Bridges', a road that follows the original route of the line as it turned east under a road overbridge. Today, an exclusive housing development occupies the former trackbed. *Ashley Butlin*

Heading east along the A72 the explorer soon arrives at Cardrona. Once a small village, today the location is a major residential development complete with a large golf course. Cardrona station and signal box is now Nashy's Coffee House, and remain virtually as they were when the line closed; even parts of the platform edge can still be clearly seen. Just to the right of the platform end is the remains of a concrete permanent way cabin which amazingly still stands (just!) over 60 years after the line closed. *Iona Butlin*

Innerleithen is one of the larger towns on this section of the line and was once home to a number of mills, this being reflected in a larger goods yard than most stations. Today the station building is another private residence but still clearly retains its railway origins especially with regard to the platform canopy which can be seen on the right of the building. *Iona Butlin*

Further west we arrive at Walkerburn where yet again the station building is a private residence. Located south of the River Tweed, the station was a little distance from the town. *Iona Butlin*

Lauder Branch

As the Border towns on the Waverley Route profited from the arrival of the railway, so those towns not directly served pushed to be linked to the line. Branch lines to Peebles, Jedburgh, Selkirk and Langholm resulted in them all benefitting from the new opportunities brought about by the railway with the resulting increase in prosperity. Another town wishing to join the network was Lauder. Various schemes were proposed over the years which would have linked the town to existing lines but none came to fruition. Had it not been for the introduction of the Light Railways Act of 1896 it seemed that Lauder would not get a railway. Prior to this Act, railways required lengthy planning and an Act of Parliament before work could commence. Under the new Act, designed to help railways reach rural areas particularly to allow the transportation of goods, companies were able to obtain a Light Railway Order and construct and run a line. Limitations of the Act meant weight limits of 12 tonnes per axle and a maximum speed of 25mph, but these allowed the use of lightly laid track and structures designed to keep costs lower.

On 5 June 1898 a new company was formed to build and run a line from Fountainhall to Oxton and Lauder. In a ceremony at the site of Lauder station on 3 June 1899 the first sod was cut and construction was underway. Progress was rapid but bad winter weather slowed work and further delays followed in 1900 so the line wasn't completed until the summer of 1901. At 10½ miles in length, there was one intermediate station at Oxton, and the line followed a circuitous route around Collie Law, approaching Lauder from the north west. Passenger numbers were steady and with goods traffic the line was considered a success. Inward, the line brought tourists especially for trout fishing and walking.

At the amalgamation on 1 January 1923, the Lauder Light Railway along with the North British Railway came under the auspices of the London & North Eastern Railway (LNER). While the line gave a link to Edinburgh by changing at Fountainhall, the journey was protracted and not particularly user friendly. When a bus service commenced in 1924 between Lauder and Edinburgh it proved a great success, and although the railway continued in profit the writing was on the wall. Passenger services ceased on 10 September 1932.

The line remained open for goods traffic although road competition here also had an impact. A boost came to the line for a short while during the Second World War with the construction of a large food depot next to the station run by the Ministry of Food, the location being considered a safe location away from bombers. Goods traffic finally ended on 3 September 1958.

Hidden amongst the trees and bushes alongside the A7, the bridge that carried the Lauder branch over the Gala Water still remains in place. *Iona Butlin*

Like Lauder, Oxton also had a station for just 31 years from 1901–1932. The station site has been cleared but the station-master's house remains in private ownership. To the side of the property remains an LNER Trespass notice. The line and station were located to the right of the house. *Iona Butlin*

A Branch Line Society rail tour to Lauder on 15 November 1958 was hauled by BR Standard No 78049, seen here running round its coaches at Lauder. The food depot is in the background. *Hamish Stevenson*

Lauder station opened on 2 July 1901 and closed to passengers on 12 September 1932 but remained open to goods traffic until October 1938. At the start of the Second World War the Ministry of Food opened a food buffer depot to supply valuable food supplies around the country should the need arise. The rural location was considered safe from enemy bombers. Following closure of the line, whilst all evidence of the station has disappeared the food store buildings remain in private ownership. *Iona Butlin*

Selkirk Branch

Due to the topography of the Southern Uplands, the Edinburgh & Hawick Railway bypassed Selkirk, being routed for Galashiels via Melrose and St Boswells on its way to Hawick. Consequently the Selkirk & Galashiels Railway was instigated in 1854 and worked in agreement with the NBR. It was constructed as a 5¼-mile branch from Galashiels which followed the River Tweed through to Selkirk, the line opening on 5 April 1856. It was absorbed by the NBR in 1859. The branch left the Waverley Route at Selkirk Junction just north of the Redbridge Viaduct leading to the first station at Abbotsford Ferry, on the opposite bank to Abbotsford House. From here a ferry connected the station to the former home of Sir Walter Scott (novelist, playwright and poet 1771-1832). The station opened in May 1856 a month after passenger services commenced, closing on 1 May 1931.

Crossing the River Tweed, the next station was at Lindean where a goods yard served a small community. The station closed to passengers on 10 September 1951, while it remained open to goods until 23 March 1964.

Situated alongside the River Tweed, Boleside was the location for Abbotsford Ferry station on the Selkirk branch. From here visitors could be ferried across the river to Abbotsford House. The station closed in May 1931 but remained open for excursion traffic especially linked to the Galashiels Common Riding, through to the late 1950s. *Bruce McCartney collection*

A wonderful view south of Boleside of the Selkirk branch showing the line sweeping around to cross the River Tweed. The A7 trunk road heads to the right before also crossing the river behind the trees. Following closure of the branch major realignment of the road saw the railway bridge demolished and the road built on the trackbed through to Lindean and beyond. *Bruce McCartney collection*

The station at Selkirk opened on 5 April 1856 in what was described as a 'rural setting'. The arrival of the railway heralded a growth in mills alongside the railway and the Ettrick Water. Photographed on 10 July 1950 just over a year before passenger services ceased, the general layout of the station area shows the single platform on the left and the goods yard centre and right. The whole site is now completely cleared of railway infrastructure and is home to the Scottish Borders Housing Association, but many of the mills remain either derelict or in different usage. Evidence of the former railway includes the Station Hotel and Level Crossing Road a little way down the line from the station site. *George Ellis, Hamish Stevenson Collection*

Selkirk is another Borders town where mills dominated the life of the community with many involved either directly or indirectly with the wool trade. The station, which terminated on South Bridge Street, had a single platform, along with a relatively extensive goods yard. Passenger services ceased on 10 September 1951, with goods traffic ending on 2 November 1964.

Langholm Branch

At seven miles in length, the Langholm branch opened in April 1864. Leaving Riddings Junction just north of the station the track crossed the Liddel Water on a skew nine-arch viaduct and crossed the border and entered Scotland. At just under two miles from Riddings, Canonbie was the first village and the line actually opened to here in May 1862 to serve a colliery owned by the Duke of Buccleuch. Interestingly, Canonbie was another location to have its name changed, having opened as Canobie; it was renamed on 1 February 1904.

Marking the site of Langholm station just off the A7 is a plaque and information board. Housing has been built on much of the station site. *Iona Butlin*

The picturesque location of Canonbie station on 16 July 1962 as No 43139 waits to depart to Riddings Junction.
Bruce McCartney collection

Just a mile beyond Canonbie lay Gilnockie, another rural location, reports of which indicate only limited use over the years.

Terminating at Langholm, the branch served yet another town known for its tweed mills. The station was provided with a covered platform and goods depot and yard, in addition to an engine shed which remained in use until May 1932. Opened on 18 April 1864 the station remained in use until it closed on 15 June 1964. Goods facilities ceased on 18 September 1967.

British Railways
Scottish and London Midland Regions

TRANSPORT ACT. 1962
WITHDRAWAL OF
RAILWAY PASSENGER SERVICES

The British Railways Board hereby give notice, in accordance with Section 56 (7) of the Transport Act, 1962, that on and from 9th September, 1963, they propose to discontinue the local railway passenger services

BETWEEN

LANGHOLM
AND
CARLISLE
AND FROM
LANGHOLM, GILNOCKIE, CANONBIE and RIDDINGS JCT. STATIONS

It appears to the Board that the following alternative services will be available:—

Omnibus services operated by WESTERN S.M.T. COMPANY LTD. (Tables Nos. 215, 226), SCOTTISH OMNIBUSES LTD. (Tables Nos. 55, 56) and RIBBLE MOTOR SERVICES LTD., between Langholm and Carlisle via Gilnockie and Canonbie provide 6 buses to Carlisle and 7 from Carlisle daily Mondays to Fridays and 11 each way on Saturdays with a time interval between buses of from 5 minutes to 4 hours.

An assurance has been given that, if required and subject to the authority of the Traffic Commissioners, road passenger services can be augmented between Langholm and Carlisle.

Any user of the rail service it is proposed to withdraw and any body representing such users, desirous of objecting to the proposal, may lodge objections within six weeks of 28th JUNE, 1963, i.e. not later than 10th AUGUST, 1963.

Users who wish to make representations in respect of that part of the line which is in the County of Dumfries, including Langholm, Gilnockie and Canonbie stations, should address such objections to the Secretary of the Transport Users' Consultative Committee for Scotland at 39 George Street, Edinburgh, 2, and those wishing to make representations concerning that part of the service which is in the County of Cumberland, including Riddings Junction Station, should address any objections to the Secretary of the Transport Users' Consultative Committee for the North Western Area at Peter House, 2 Oxford Street, Manchester, 1.

NOTE—If any objections are lodged within the period specified above, the closure cannot be proceeded with until the Transport Users' Consultative Committees have reported to the Minister and the Minister has given his consent (Section 56 (8) of the Transport Act, 1962).

Bruce McCartney

Regular branch locomotive Ivatt 2-6-0 No 43139 off Carlisle Canal shed waits at Langholm station to depart for Riddings Junction on 16 July 1962, two years before the line closed to passenger traffic. *Bruce McCartney collection*

Gretna Branch

Gretna is located on the West Coast Main Line (WCML) although the present day Gretna station is actually on the Glasgow & South Western line to Dumfries, the former Caledonian Gretna station on the WCML closing in 1951.

The NBR constructed a short branch from the south end of Longtown station through to Gretna where they built a station alongside the existing Caledonian station. Opened on 1 November 1861 it closed on 9 August 1915 but re-opened for goods on 16 August 1923, remaining open until 10 September 1951. In 1963 a south facing junction was installed linking the branch to the WCML so allowing up trains to run direct from the Waverley Route at Longtown through to the marshalling yard at Kingmoor via the WCML, thus avoiding unnecessary reversal moves south of the yard.

Associated with the military establishments in the area was the construction of MoD Longtown in 1915, largely to the south of the Gretna branch, along with the smaller Smalmstown base north of the line and the A6071 road. It was this latter location with its many rail-linked ammunition bunkers that was used in recent years for the storage of locomotives and coaching stock which could be viewed both from the A6071 and A7 roads. More recently, the site was disconnected from the main base and is no longer rail linked. A local farmer has utilised the trackbed for a new farm entrance in addition to constructing new barns on the trackbed.

Within the main depot, an extensive rail system remains linked to the WCML and receives MoD trains from various other MoD sites in the country. The line beyond the MoD depot to Longtown closed on 31 August 1970.

The Gretna branch runs through what is now MoD Longtown, making photographs very difficult to obtain. However, this was the view in September 2016 of a level crossing over the line just inside the perimeter fence at one of the lesser used entrances to the site. *Iona Butlin*

The station building at Gretna survives and is now the farmhouse for a large concern that has buildings on the railway yard and trackbed. *Iona Butlin*

Rebuilding the Borders Railway

When the final passenger train travelled south in January 1969 amid protest and ensuing media hype, few could imagine that almost 50 years later trains would once again climb Falahill, or hear an announcement at Edinburgh Waverley that 'the train standing at Platform xx was bound for Galashiels'.

In the following years an abortive attempt was made to preserve the line in its entirety that sadly came to naught. After the collapse of the preservation scheme, track lifting quickly followed in earnest, being completed in 1972. Following the cessation of coal traffic out of Lady Victoria Colliery which had continued on a single track to Millerhill Yard from 1969 to 28 July 1972, this too was lifted. In addition to track lifting a number of structures including Hawick station which later became the site of a Leisure Centre were demolished. Thankfully, the vast majority of structures including the impressive Lothianbridge Viaduct remained in place. With the removal of track, nature began to reclaim the route. In rural areas, farmers made use of the trackbed to facilitate easy movement around their farms. In addition, due to the hard standing of the ballast, it made excellent feeding areas for cattle and sheep. In other places, especially in the areas around Eskbank and Galashiels, the local authorities took over the route and laid tarmac to make cycleways and footpaths.

In 1999, 40 years after the line closed, the Scottish Executive commissioned a feasibility study into the re-opening of the Waverley Route from Edinburgh Waverley to Carlisle. For those who had campaigned for the re-opening of the route almost from the day it closed, this was just the news that they wanted to hear and raised the possibility that the route could be revived. In the study was a recommendation that a line be built from Edinburgh to the Central Borders. Following on from this in 2003 the Waverley Bill was lodged with the Scottish Parliament. It was the Scottish Borders Council that took the lead to promote the Bill.

Three years later on 24 July 2006 the Bill was given Royal Assent and became the Waverley Railway (Scotland) Act 2006. Following this, a ceremony took place at Galashiels when the then Minister for Transport and Infrastructure, Stewart Stevenson, cut a sod to commence the building of the line.

Two years later in 2008 Transport Scotland assumed responsibility of the newly renamed Borders Railway. Meanwhile, detailed plans were drawn up for the complete rebuilding of the railway covering every aspect of the project, from the alignment of tracks to the size and height of lineside fencing, so as to allow an accurate tendering of the scheme. All of these plans were available on the website for the general public to view.

Out among the hills near Whitrope summit with track lifting well under way. *Bruce McCartney collection*

Situated just beyond Bowshank Tunnel, and clearly visible from the A7 road in the summer of 2000, was this 'straw locomotive' built by a local farmer on the former trackbed – a foresight of what was to appear a number of years later. *Jenny Butlin*

Transport Scotland required a company to construct the new line but struggled to get firms to tender within budget. In the event, Network Rail was chosen in 2011 to be responsible for delivering the railway, led by project director Hugh Wark who was to become a familiar figure over the coming years as the project advanced.

The project was signed over to Network Rail on 6 November 2012 in a meeting at the National Mining Museum, Newtongrange. Among the benefits highlighted which the new railway would bring was that it would significantly contribute to the area's economy, especially by acting as a catalyst for business development and new housing within easy commuting distance of Edinburgh. A new public transport link from the Borders and Midlothian was estimated to cut road use by as much as 60,000 trips per year so reducing carbon emissions and making both the A7 and A68 safer.

It was not only the construction of the railway but also the rebuilding of existing roads and new ones that was involved in the project. At Galashiels, the Inner Relief Road underwent considerable changes as early as 2011 both to accommodate the new transport interchange in Stirling Street for bus and rail, and to allow for easier movement of traffic through the town on the A7 road. The cost of the road works at Galashiels was put at £1.44 million shared between the Scottish Borders Council (SBC) and the Scottish Government. Throughout the construction of the railway, the SBC backed the projects, and the council leader David Parker was very much a leading supporter.

In December 2012 Network Rail announced that it had appointed construction agency BAM Nuttall as the main contractor for the building of the Borders Railway. The choice of BAM Nuttall made sense as Network Rail had been working closely in the previous months with BAM to draw up the initial designs for the new line.

Although in general the Borders Railway followed the original course of the Waverley Route, a deviation was made south of Newcraighall station to avoid passing through Millerhill Marshalling Yard. Instead, the line went through the site of the former Monktonhall colliery, rejoining the original route south of the City Bypass near Sheriffhall. This deviation was in connection with the Shawfair development which will see 4,000 homes being built here in the coming years.

Passing through the colliery site required considerable stabilisation of the ground due to the former mine workings which required filling in or being stabilised. Commencing after the start of October 2012, this work was to take six months to complete before building the railway could commence. Also, in July 2012, one of the first 'casualties' of the old Waverley Route was the footbridge at Eskbank station which connected the two platforms and had remained in place since the closure. This was carefully removed and donated to the Waverley Route Heritage Association located at Whitrope for restoration.

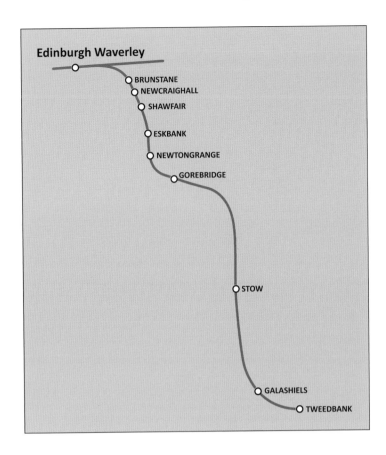

Following the appointment of BAM Nuttall, work began in earnest at the start of 2013 on advanced preparations prior to the main building/construction commencing in March.

In connection with these works, footpaths/cycle ways in Midlothian were progressively closed from mid-February starting at Sheriffhall and Gorebridge. The number of key pedestrian points crossing the route was maintained as far as possible with alternatives made where necessary. It was this closure of these well used off-road routes that was the first real tangible evidence that construction work was about to begin.

A further obvious sign of the start of construction in early 2013 was the second stage of vegetation removal, especially at Hardengreen, Fountainhall and Falahill where new roads were to be built. De-vegetation opened up a safe working area for the construction teams to get on with their work.

One of the key 'selling points' of the new railway was that local employers would benefit from its construction both with the actual building and the knock-on effects of the railway with regard to tourism and the impact on local businesses. In February 2013 BAM hosted a meeting at the National Mining Museum, Scotland at Newtongrange attended by over 200 local companies from across Edinburgh, Midlothian and the Scottish Borders, giving them the opportunity to learn more about the process involved in becoming a supplier to the project.

Following the second stage of vegetation removal in early 2013, work commenced in late March with the major removal of many thousands of tonnes of spoil required to clear the route prior to tracklaying. Initially this was limited to the northern end of the line in Midlothian. By May, work was underway throughout the length of the line which in places

Looking south towards Millerhill Yard, the line to the Borders Railway goes off to the right. Formerly this was a turn-back siding for trains running through to Newcraighall station behind the photographer. This marked the start of the deviation of the new line towards Shawfair station; the former Waverley Route went straight ahead through Millerhill Yard.
Iona Butlin

became very evident to members of the public. Amongst the most obvious locations were the underpass on the City Bypass, the new viaduct across Hardengreen roundabout, the overbridge at Gore Glen, the crossing at Falahill and the new road accesses to Fountainhall and Heriot.

It was realised that the construction would impact on communities in terms of greatly increased road traffic and noise from machinery involved with re-excavating cuttings and embankments following over 50 years of neglect. Knowing that the work on building the Borders Railway could not go ahead without significant disruption to the lives of many people, Network Rail and BAM pledged to do all they could to keep disturbance to a minimum and asked for patience and understanding during the construction phase.

By April 2013 the project was divided into three sections: Northern, Central and Southern, with bases at Newtongrange, Fountainhall and Galashiels for each of the areas.

Following on from the initial preparatory works, the main construction commenced on 18 April involving the excavation of the new track alignment from Newcraighall through the Monktonhall area, and excavation of the new Shawfair station.

Although considerable remedial work took place in the Monktonhall area where 4,000 tonnes of grout had been pumped into old mine workings, further consolidation was required at both Eskbank and Newtongrange where mining over the years had caused subsidence and underground voids which needed to be filled prior to the track being laid.

Unfortunately when the City Bypass was constructed in the 1980s, no provision was made for the rebuilding of the railway – understandable given the attitude to rail at the time. Consequently, a new crossing was required and this took the form of an underpass east of Sheriffhall Roundabout and involved constructing a temporary diversion to the north of the bypass while the engineers built a new bridge to allow the line to run under the bypass. Work commenced building the diversion in June 2013, and with traffic diverted from September 2013, was completed in June 2014.

Approximately 1.5 million tonnes of spoil had to be excavated in the building of the line with approximately 330,000 cubic yards of soil to be moved in the Shawfair area alone. Other areas with large excavations included Eskbank, Newtongrange, Falahill and Galashiels. All of this brought numerous lorries onto the A7 and surrounding roads. Where possible, lorries utilised the trackbed including that over the Lothianbridge Viaduct. The viaduct was built back in 1847 and was a convenient route for some 10,000 cubic yards of soil to be transported between Newtongrange and the new embankment being built for the Hardengreen Viaduct so avoiding unnecessary lorries on the adjoining road.

Among the other signs of construction, piling was taking place at both Hardengreen and Gore Glen where new bridges were being built across the A7 road, starting in July. For those travelling on the A7, the former station at Fountainhall took on a new appearance in the summer of

Looking north along the trackbed in February 2013, Lady Victoria Colliery was to the right, with the National Mining Museum, Scotland visible in the distance. *Iona Butlin*

An early view of Gorebridge station in April 2013 before serious reconstruction took place but after a number of recently built houses in the former goods yard in the foreground had been demolished and the site cleared. *Iona Butlin*

Known either as Lothianbridge or Newbattle Viaduct, the vast structure is situated south of Hardengreen. The 14 spans cross the South Esk River 80 feet above the water. Thankfully, this Grade B listed structure was not demolished following the closure of the railway in 1969. This view was taken on the trackbed on 25 April 2013 before the site was closed off to allow construction work to commence. As is often the case with such structures, unless one knows where to look, passengers on the line are probably unaware of the location as their trains cross the imposing bridge. *Iona Butlin*

2013 with the arrival of numerous portakabins which formed the new central hub offices. At 20 miles in length between Catcune Farm and Bowland Estate, the central section was the longest, running through a predominantly rural setting. The site was officially opened on 24 June 2013 by Simon Walton and Tom Curry from the Campaign for Borders Rail and became the base for 70 staff responsible for the central section.

In April 2013, following tree clearance, work has commenced on building the new piers to carry the new Gore Glen Bridge over the A7 road. *Iona Butlin*

Falahill is the highest point on the line and, in the past, the A7 crossed the railway on an overbridge (see picture on page 13). Following closure, the opportunity was taken to remove the bridge and re-align the road. This photograph taken in 2013 shows the location prior to major construction work completely changed the view. *Iona Butlin*

Activity reached Galashiels and Tweedbank in July 2013 with the closure of roads and foothpaths. Plumtreehall Brae linking Magdala Terrace and King Street was closed from the middle of the month as the road bridge over the line was not high enough to give clearance for the reconstructed line. The former bridge was demolished and replaced by a new footbridge. At the same time, the Black Path for pedestrians and cyclists between Glenfield Road and Winston Road was closed in stages to allow construction to take place. The remaining section between Winston Road and Tweedbank over the Redbridge Viaduct was to remain open for longer, although the section near the proposed entrance to Tweedbank station was closed to allow access to the site.

In August 2013, Network Rail submitted new plans for a redesigned road layout at Falahill. Originally, a small bridge crossed the line at Falahill on a sharp bend but after the line closed the opportunity was taken to re-align the road and remove the dog-legged bridge. Initial plans submitted for the railway included two roundabouts and a bridge at Falahill cottages. This was later amended following discussions with the local residents resulting in a re-alignment of both the A7 and the railway, removing the need for roundabouts and so keeping traffic flowing freely on the A7.

One of the biggest engineering projects on the line was the construction of a new bridge to carry the railway over Hardengreen Roundabout. When viewed in January 2014 the three piers had been constructed in preparation for the deck girders to be installed. *Iona Butlin*

The summer of 2013 was fairly settled weather-wise allowing good progress to be made along the 30-mile length of the railway. Work was progressing well at Shawfair station where earthworks saw over 500,000 tonnes of soil removed from the site, some of which was taken to build the temporary diversion on the city bypass.

Heading south, the work at Hardengreen Roundabout was progressing with utility services being relocated prior to building the centre pier in the middle of the roundabout. Just beyond, contractors worked on repairs to Lothianbridge Viaduct including re-pointing the old stonework. Repairs to the viaduct were undertaken by Midlothian-based stonemasons Forth Stone from Bonnyrigg. In addition to re-pointing the

stonework, the company also replaced defective masonry. At Gore Glen piling of the new overbridge was completed during July. Falahill had a large quarry opened to the east of the line to provide rocks for the new roads being constructed at Heriot and Fountainhall.

Bowshank Tunnel was sealed by this time to allow structural work to be undertaken. Excavations at Tweedbank resulted in a large pile of earth being visible, this ultimately being used to build a new embankment near Currie Road in Galashiels.

With the approaching autumn, in September 2013 motorists using the A720 City Bypass were made very aware of the new railway in the vicinity of Sheriffhall roundabout when a temporary diversion of the dual carriageway road was gradually brought to use over a three-week programme which allowed a section of the existing road to be excavated for the building of a bridge over the new railway. Once traffic was using the temporary diversion, work rapidly progressed to cut away the existing road to allow the construction of the new bridge. Many motorists would probably have been unaware of the reason for their 40mph diversion off the existing route.

Along the length of the line, many of the 200 original bridges were to be refurbished and re-used – a real tribute to the Victorian craftsmen who installed them approximately 165 years ago. Existing iron girder bridges being reused had to be grit blasted and repaired, the work taking place within white encapsulated 'tunnels'. These were very visible during the autumn/winter of 2013 for those travelling on the nearby A7 road. Another area highly visible to motorists was the large quarry opened at Falahill to provide essential rocks for construction sites. From early September, for 14 weeks daily at approximately 13.45, controlled blasting by specialists saw the closure of the A7 for around ten minutes as a safety precaution in the unlikely event of material being thrown onto the road. Residents at Falahill cottages and workers at the quarry received a five-minute warning siren followed by a one-minute siren prior to blasting taking place.

From September 2013, Winston Road in Galashiels was closed for the following 12 months to allow significant work to be taken place. Following the closure of the line in 1969, the bridge over the track in Winston Road became redundant, and the arch was filled with concrete, and the road rebuilt over the top. In addition, much of the old cutting at this point was infilled over the years. All of this infill had to be removed along with the old bridge prior to a new one being constructed and the track re-laid at the correct level as the line passed over the Redbridge Viaduct.

One major obstacle to the new line was the A720 Edinburgh City bypass. In order to pass under the road, a diversion was constructed so allowing the contractors to construct a new underbridge. When complete the former road layout was restored and the diversion returned to agricultural use. *Photo courtesy of Network Rail*

A large quarry was opened up at Falahill to provide much needed stone for the rebuilding work. Viewed on 1 November 2013 the scale of the work is clear to those travelling by on the adjacent A7 road. *Iona Butlin*

Rainfall has a significant effect on the terrain of the Scottish Borders and marshy areas are common not only in the hills but also at lower levels. Some sections of the route were more prone to the effect of water egress than others, Tynehead being particularly vulnerable with resultant landslides. When rebuilding, the cutting here received special attention using tried and tested engineering techniques to limit landslides. In the past, many repairs were made in the area and so the embankments required reconstructing with rock-filled drains and a covering of a rock blanket, all of which should minimise the potential for landslides. Carried out in the late summer and autumn of 2013, this essential ground work to bring the railway up to 21st century standards needed to be completed before the new trackbed could be laid and involved practically rebuilding the old Tynehead cuttings to ensure that the water drained away through new channels.

The cutting at Tynehead was particularly prone to flooding and potential landslides. Prior to any significant work commencing at the location when viewed in August 2013, the hazard potential is evident. *Iona Butlin*

Construction of stone drainage and consolidation of the unstable embankments at Tynehead – 1 November 2013.
Iona Butlin

As summer turned to autumn in 2013, work was at full pace along the whole length of the railway with approximately 1,000 people employed on the project. At the northern end, construction was progressing well at the site of the City Bypass, with the old road excavated, construction of the box bridge the next development awaited. Construction consisted of 48 22-tonne wall panels and 24 66-tonne road panels which would allow the railway to run below the City Bypass. In addition, the bridge was constructed to allow for the potential re-building in the future of the Sheriffhall roundabout, a current bottleneck on the bypass.

At both Hardengreen and Gore Glen piling work was all but completed and supports for the new bridges taking shape. Further south, refurbishment of the old metal bridges progressed with a number encapsulated in white tents to allow grit blasting to safely take place prior to repairs and repainting. In addition, a number of new concrete bridges, some large, as at Heriot and Fountainhall, and other smaller occupation underbridges both for farmers and small burns, were constructed. At Heriot and Fountainhall the former level crossings were being replaced by bridges, both requiring considerable groundworks with an impact on the adjacent A7 road with significant speed restrictions and delays. One such bridge at Rye Haugh Water north of Galashiels, where the original bridge deck was removed following the closure of the Waverley Route, had a new deck

installed in September/October involving a 450-tonne crane lifting four 20-tonne concrete beams onto the original bridge abutments which had been repaired and repointed. The actual lift took just one day and was indicative of the efforts made by the work force throughout the project to ensure that it was brought in on time.

In connection with bridge building, the A7 was closed in early November to allow 15 large precast concrete beams to be lifted into place across the road, so forming the deck of the new railway bridge at Gore Glen. The following week the A7 was again closed for a day at Gore Glen to allow the concrete to be poured to form the bridge deck.

Reference has already been made to the possibilities of harsh winters in the Scottish Borders. The winter of 2013-14 was faced with some trepidation by BAM, not knowing exactly how the weather would impact on construction works. Even in an average winter, the short day length, rainfall and general freezing conditions all impact on construction work. For motorists travelling the A7 and on the many side roads around the railway mud on the road was a significant factor and in an attempt to keep the roads as mud-free as possible a fleet of 11 road sweepers became a regular sight. In addition, vehicles passed through mobile wheel wash facilities at those locations where mud was particularly prevalent. In addition, major earthworks were scaled back to minimise potential disruption on the A7 and surrounding roads during the winter months.

When viewed in August 2013 the original platforms at Heriot remained in place awaiting removal as work on the route progressed. *Iona Butlin*

In the past, level crossings at Fountainhall and Heriot didn't prove a problem. In today's railways, level crossings are a hindrance to road and rail traffic, and dangerous for perambulating humans and animals. In addition, they are costly to operate and maintain. Consequently at both Fountainhall and Heriot new road overbridges were built along with improvements to the adjacent A7 road. When viewed in January 2014 work was well under way with the bridge box complete and the associated road works taking shape. *Iona Butlin*

Motorists using the A7 in the Gorebridge area would have watched the new bridge at Gore Glen progress steadily during 2013–14 to the point in April 2014 when it was all but complete ready for track laying. *Iona Butlin*

The first railway bridge to be restored, Crookston Mill Railway Bridge, across the Gala Water north of Fountainhall, was unwrapped in December 2013. Taking five months to strengthen and grit blast prior to finishing in 'Holly Green' paint, the 150-year-old structure looked resplendent and a tribute both to the original builders and the present team. The colour was chosen to blend in with the environment.

Twelve similar wrought-iron girder bridges were all subject to the same treatment.

Between October 2013 and January 2014 the first phase of refurbishing Bowshank Tunnel was completed with the masonry repaired where required. Phase two involved the lowering of the floor by 40cm to allow installation of the track slabs.

In order to refurbish a number of the cast iron bridges they were encapsulated in white plastic sheet to both contain the grit blasting required to remove old paint and rust, and to provide a dry environment for repairs and repainting to take place. This particular example between Fountainhall and Heriot was photographed in November 2013. *Iona Butlin*

One of the biggest engineering projects on the line was the construction of a new bridge to carry the railway over Hardengreen Roundabout. A visit in January 2014 found that the three piers had been constructed in preparation for the deck girders to be installed. By the end of February 2014 the bridge deck was in place and the side walls to the rail deck were being installed. *Iona Butlin*

As 2014 commenced, so work increased. The weather held fine allowing good progress to be made. One of the most significant structures on the railway is the new bridge at Hardengreen Roundabout. Here, the embankment of the former Waverley Route was removed when new roads were built following its closure in 1969. Over the weekend of 15-16 February 2015 the roads in and around the vicinity of Hardengreen Roundabout were all closed for the major lift of four 107-tonne concrete beams to be lifted in to place to form the 71.5m new bridge. Employing a 1,200-tonne crane, a 30-strong construction team worked through from 22.00 on the Friday to 06.00 on the Monday to see the vital stage of the project progress as the longest new structure on the railway took shape. The lift followed seven months of preparatory construction work of the supporting piers on which the large beams rest.

The next phase of the build followed over the weekend of 1-2 March, when a second complete road closure occurred to allow the 30 precast bridge girders to be lifted into place on the four concrete beams. Once in place the reinforced concrete bridge deck could be cast in situ using 350 tonnes of concrete.

Another of the former structures being re-used is the Redbridge Viaduct across the River Tweed between Galashiels and Tweedbank. Since the closure of the Waverley Route, the trackbed was converted to a cycle/footpath linking Melrose, Tweedbank and Galashiels, and has been a popular route for many people. On inspection, initially the bridge was found to be in excellent condition and only minimal structural repairs thought to be required for the new line. In February 2014, the bridge was closed for eight weeks to allow essential repairs including waterproofing the deck prior to resurfacing. With the line now being single track across the bridge, the footpath was re-instated alongside the line, the path protected from the trains by fencing. However, when work commenced on the bridge it was discovered that it was not as good as first thought with previous repairs inconsistent and in need of considerably more remedial action than initially predicted. Consequently the work on the bridge required the footpath to be closed for a further 10 weeks.

In the Shawfair area, starting 3 March 2014, the A6106 had to be re-aligned to allow the diverted line through the area. The road was closed for six months between Millerhill and the Sheriffhall roundabout. The new alignment for the railway cuts through the former A6106.

By spring 2014 the construction of two new bridges serving Fountainhall and Heriot off the A7 was progressing well, along with works on the A7 to improve access to the new roads. Traffic control on the A7 at these locations caused some disruption to drivers who were advised to make use of the nearby A68 where possible. Next in line was the construction of the new overbridge at Falahill which brought further delays to traffic on the A7.

Galashiels is the most populated of the towns on the railway and, although the trackbed was virtually intact, considerable works were required to bring it up to present day requirements including increasing clearance on bridges to accommodate modern lorries – considerably larger than those on the roads in the 1960s. Two new structures were required to cross Wheatlands Road and Currie Road, while a third bridge crossed the Gala Water.

It was very fortunate that a number of key structures remained in place following closure of the Waverley Route. Among these was the Redbridge Viaduct over the River Tweed between Galashiels and Tweedbank. *Iona Butlin*

It was not only major bridges that required repair and/or rebuilding but also small farm crossings such as here north of Galashiels where considerable work was being undertaken on 11 January 2014. *Iona Butlin*

Threading the railway through the Plumtree Brae area in the north of Galashiels was always complex with railway bridges over roads and water, while a road bridge passed over the track at a higher level. To increase clearance over Wheatlands Road the track level was raised resulting in a new bridge being built over the Gala Water while Plumtreehall Brae Road was closed to cars and rebuilt as a footbridge. These two views show the new bridge over Wheatlands Road and the work being undertaken at Plumtree Brae in April 2014. *Iona Butlin*

As mentioned previously in the history of the line, at Bowland, instead of a level crossing, an underbridge for the road was constructed for the safety of children reaching the A7. This bridge had limited height clearance and with the reconstruction, the opportunity was taken to remove the original structure and replace it with a new bridge with increased clearance, the trackbed being raised either side of the bridge to allow this to take place. The former bridge deck was dismantled during 2013.

Occasionally during a project of this size it is inevitable that unforeseen problems arise. One such event was the Borthwick Road bridge which, while initially thought solid, was discovered to have cracks following excavation work prior to the installation of gabion baskets to strengthen the cutting. As a result the road had to be closed from 14 May to the end of July while remedial work was undertaken.

Whilst every effort was made throughout construction to keep disruption to members of the public to a minimum, it was inevitable that road closures and diversions could not be avoided. Some were quite lengthy, but others very short lived lasting only a matter of days. Where possible these took place overnight or at weekends especially where they impacted on businesses. Of the bridges in Galashiels, that at Wheatlands Road required a weekend closure in early May for the lifting of the 90-tonne bridge into place using a 500-tonne crane and a 15-strong work force. Further south on the other side of Galashiels, the bridge at Currie Road was more complex and required a road closure of around four weeks from mid May to mid June.

A press release in early 2014, 12 months after work commenced, gave the following facts and figures:

'Among their achievements in the last year, those workers have:

Moved 804,000 tonnes of earth Used 400 tonnes of grouting as part of mining remediation work Installed 25.6 km of drainage works

Worked on 104 bridges including 12 footbridges, 39 overbridges and 53 underbridges

Installed 22,800 m³ of gabion baskets to support embankments and cuttings

Since the start of the project, Network Rail and principal contractor BAM have also actively engaged with over 3,000 members of the local communities along the line of the route at local events and community meetings. They have also responded to 1,500 specific enquiries and reached over 140,000 unique visitors via the project website.

Keeping the project team fuelled has been a logistical challenge in itself and an estimated 25,000 bacon rolls from local caterers have helped to keep construction crews energised.'

In May 2014, 220 students from Germany, The Netherlands, France, Denmark and Latvia attending Edinburgh Napier University's International Project Week were given a tour of Shawfair. During the visit they were given practical demonstrations of the building of platforms and footbridges at Shawfair along with the construction of the new access road.

Following closure of the Waverley Route in 1969, a number of bridges over minor roads were demolished to allow easier access. One such bridge was at Bowland. This was a particularly low bridge that had originally been planned to be a level crossing but changed to a bridge to allow easy access for school children to the A7. At this point the trackbed was significantly raised to allow a new bridge to be constructed with sufficient clearance for today's vehicles. *Iona Butlin*

When viewed on 28 June 2014, the station at Shawfair was beginning to take shape although much work still remained to be undertaken. *Iona Butlin*

By the summer of 2014 the vast piles of soil previously at Tweedbank had been moved to create new embankments in Galashiels and the site levelled in preparation for the building of the station platforms and large car park. *Iona Butlin*

In early June 2014 construction of the City Bypass overbridge reached completion and during the first week of the month, traffic was reinstated along the original route of the A720, allowing the short diversion around the construction site to be removed.

Over the weekend of 30 May–2 June the new 30-tonne bridge was installed at Plumtreehall Brae using a 500-tonne crane, necessitating the closure of a number of local roads. Disruption was kept to a minimum to avoid inconveniencing members of the public. On the other side of the town, in early June 2014, Currie Road was re-opened following the installation of the new bridge deck over the road.

Located in Ladhope Vale, the new station in Galashiels consists of a single platform in a tight corridor between the road and a large retaining wall. In order for construction to commence in July 2014 a one-way road system was implemented to allow partial closure of the road whilst construction took place between July and early December.

One of the many minor roads temporarily closed during the construction of the railway, the B710 road at Bowland re-opened in July 2014 following a three-month closure and the rebuilding of the bridge.

By the summer of 2014 with less than one year before the railway was due for completion, attention was turning to building stations with both Shawfair and Eskbank making progress. Along the route progress was good with work on new bridges all but complete. The track route was now well defined and the laying of sleepers was imminent ahead of the arrival of the track-laying machine.

In August, installation of fencing along the route of the line commenced, along with further clearance of vegetation to allow safe use of the line and clear visibility for the train drivers. Construction of station platforms and footbridges progressed southwards and by October had reached Newtongrange, Gorebridge and Stow. Work at Falahill was complete in October and the new road opened, along with the new link road to Heriot. A further new access road was opened by the beginning of November, namely to Fountainhall. Both this and the road to Heriot replaced level crossings on the former Waverley Route. Also at Fountainhall, the new road link is equipped with a footpath linking Fountainhall with the bus stop located on the nearby A7, while at Heriot an underpass was constructed under the railway also to give villagers direct access to buses on the A7.

Linked with the station at Galashiels is the new bus/rail interchange building allowing easy access between the two forms of transport as well as convenient access to the town centre. Construction was well under way in September 2014 while the route of the railway to the right is taking shape. *Iona Butlin*

Considerable difficulties were faced with construction at Newtongrange due to the wet conditions. These had been resolved by September 2014 when construction of the platform was underway. *Iona Butlin*

Snow lingered on the ground at Gorebridge station on 20 January 2015 where the platform was in place, and work going ahead with the car park being constructed where the homes had been demolished several years earlier. *Iona Butlin*

In Galashiels alongside Ladhope Vale by the railway, a new retaining wall was built to support the trackbed. This was later faced with stonework to match surrounding structures.

During the autumn of 2014, work commenced to install a network of communication masts along the route, so allowing drivers to communicate with signallers and controllers. A total of 15 masts were installed at strategic locations along the line to allow optimal effectiveness of operations.

In December, further work on the Redbridge Viaduct involved the surfacing of the footpath, construction of a fence between the path and the railway, and the installation of street lighting. The Redbridge Viaduct had been a vital pedestrian/cycle link between Tweedbank and Galashiels for a number of years since the closure of the Waverley Route and its continued use was a fundamental asset of the new construction, and only made possible with the route being single line at this point.

As the year drew to a close, the stations at Shawfair and Eskbank were almost complete and awaiting the addition of final fixtures and fittings including ticket machines, access points and waiting shelters. All the other new stations were progressing on target.

As a way of thanking communities along the length of the line for their support and understanding during the construction period, Borders Railway backed a number of causes during Christmas 2014 including sponsoring new Christmas lights for Galashiels town centre. They also supported Cash for Kids, a charity led by Radio Borders to provide over 4,000 presents for vulnerable children in the Borders by providing a storage unit at Tweedbank where gifts could be stored while awaiting wrapping and distribution. In addition the team supported the Red Cross by raising money for food hampers and gifts for elderly people in need.

While track laying and civil engineering work was all very visible with regard to the construction of the line, less obvious was the installation of signalling and telecommunication systems. In the past, copper wire was used extensively, and still is in many parts of the country. However, it is not very reliable and, more so, the value of copper makes it an easy target for thieves especially in rural areas. In 2013-14, cable theft cost the rail industry throughout Britain over £2.5 million due to damage, delays and disruption. Consequently, fibre optic cables were the choice for the Borders Railway as they are far better conductors, and have virtually no scrap value to thieves, so reducing the risk of criminal activity causing delays to services.

As early as November 2012 the first sleepers were delivered to a site alongside the line deviation north of the City Bypass. The very first rails to be laid were the short length of track from the end of the Newcraighall turn-back towards the re-aligned route at Shawfair. Further south rails appeared in Bowshank Tunnel where sections of concrete slab track were laid in 2014. Elsewhere, ballast was being stockpiled along the route, and sleepers positioned ahead of track laying. With the station construction well underway and strengthening of embankments complete, the team were working towards track laying.

A visit to Shawfair on 27 February 2015 found building work on the station making very good progress with both platforms almost complete along with the footbridge. To the left of the site is the car park. *Iona Butlin*

During the summer of 2014 the 90,000 sleepers began to be unloaded at strategic points along the route in preparation for track laying commencing later in the year. This view shows stacks on 7 September waiting laying out near Stow. *Iona Butlin*

Over 90,000 sleepers were required for the route and by the end of August 2014, 80,000 were delivered and being laid out giving the impression from a distance that trackwork was already in place. A specially designed machine was used to accurately locate the sleepers prior to track laying.

The formal launch of track laying took place on 9 October at Shawfair station with the then Transport Minister Keith Brown and Network Rail CEO Mark Carne in attendance along with media representatives including local television companies.

Track laying progressed steadily and crossed from Midlothian into the Scottish Borders on 5 November 2014 at Cakemuir Burn. This particular moment was especially poignant for Councillor David Parker, leader of Scottish Borders Council, who had campaigned hard for the re-instatement of the line to the Borders. As the track machine continued on its route south laying approximately a mile each day, so other infrastructure trains followed delivering ballast and levelling the track.

By January 2015 work at Stow station was making good progress following track laying. Both platforms were taking shape and the new footbridge installed. *Iona Butlin*

Track laying reached Stow on 24 November and the local primary school children turned out en-mass to witness the historic event. The school had been following the progress of the project very carefully and had seen the station built alongside their school. In addition, Network Rail had worked closely with the school and the wider community to underline the safety messages of living near a railway.

Sadly during November 2014, a project worker was seriously injured whilst off-loading sleepers resulting in the cessation of work while additional safety procedures were put in place. Work restarted in early December with over 75% of the track laying completed. Work took a further break over the holiday period, restarting on 5 January 2015 at Ferniehurst to cover the final five miles south through Galashiels and on to Tweedbank.

Track laying reached Galashiels in the first few days of February and large crowds gathered to watch the arrival of the train in the town. Both young and old stood alongside the route as Class 66 Nos 66761 and 66741 propelled the train towards Ladhope Vale and the new station. From old age pensioners who remembered using the Waverley Route when they were children, through to the children of today who had never seen a train on the line, excitement was high and the atmosphere tangible as the train worked its way through the town.

Track laying was officially completed on Thursday 12 February when the final length of track was clipped in place by Transport Minister Keith Brown. Arriving on board Freightliner Class 66 No 66614 at Tweedbank, the Minister said:

'It is a huge honour to put the final piece of track in place and travel on the first train to run into the Borders in almost half a century.

'This is the longest domestic railway to be built in Britain in over 100 years and is a fantastic engineering achievement for Scotland and for the rail industry. But more importantly, the Borders Railway is the realisation of a long-held aspiration that will see community links restored, local economies boosted and opportunities improved for many.

'I have no doubt that Borders Railway will be hugely successful, both in enhancing Scotland's infrastructure and transforming business opportunities along the line.'

With tracklaying complete, efforts now focussed on completing ballasting of the track which had incidentally been undertaken from the start of the tracklaying, the ballast trains following the track layers onto the line, and departing ahead of their return to Millerhill. In addition, the remaining tracks required welding before the tamping machines came on site to perfect the trackbed.

The first of the three site offices to close was that at Fountainhall in January 2015. Base to over 70 personnel associated with delivering the central section of the line between Gorebridge and Stow, it had been in operation for two years.

As track laying neared completion in February 2015, so station construction was also reaching an advanced stage. All platforms were in place and work on car parks and approach roads was progressing. Where applicable, footbridges were also nearing completion. At the south end of the line, Winston Road bridge re-opened early in the year.

Long gone are the days when trains were hand painted in basic colours! Modern technology allows for the production of multicoloured vinyl wrap for trains, the same as applied to lorry fleets. Again, not limited to sample logo designs, modern wraps can be of any design including photographic images. To promote the new Borders Railway, ScotRail-vinyled Class 170 No 170414 in a primarily blue and green vinyl depicting images largely

To promote the Borders Railway, Class 170 No 170414 was wrapped in a vinyl depicting scenes both on the Borders Railway and other significant locations in Scotland. The particular unit is one that covers a number of Scottish lines between Edinburgh, Glasgow and Fife. *Iona Butlin*

associated with Edinburgh and the Borders. Amongst the images portrayed on the train are the pandas at Edinburgh Zoo, the historic Rosslyn Chapel, and scenery from the Scottish Borders. Once again, it was Keith Brown who was involved with the unveiling of the unit at Edinburgh Waverley on 17 March 2015. Class 170 units cover all the major lines connecting Scotland's cities, so allowing the mobile advertising artwork to be seen throughout much of the country.

One of the 'jokes' of the modern railways is the much used excuse for delays due to 'leaves on the line', even though Network Rail employ a major programme each autumn to minimise the effect. Accordingly, it makes sense that much of the vegetation along the length of the Borders line was cut back to reduce the possibilities of leaves causing problems, especially at gradients, where lack of adhesion due to the leaves forming a 'paste' on the track could bring the line to a stop.

Ironically, while cutting back mature trees, thousands of new trees have been planted along the length of the line especially where they help form sound barriers or screen the railway and surroundings. The cynic may think that this is to make sure that in years to come 'leaves on the line' will forever remain an 'excuse' for delays and cancellations! Others argue it is to make photography more difficult!

The final road works were completed during March when the re-aligned/rebuilt A6106 between Sheriffhall roundabout and Millerhill was re-opened overnight on 30-31 March 2015. Due to the actual line being re-aligned from Millerhill, the A6106 needed to be re-routed, and now runs parallel to the railway.

In total 95 bridges were refurbished and 42 new bridges constructed between Edinburgh and Tweedbank. The final bridge to be completed was a footbridge at Harelaw connecting Newton Village to Shawfair station.

By the end of March, all the telecommunication masts had been installed, and the signalling system was up and running and being tested. Whilst the vast majority of earth movements were completed well ahead of track laying, the final moves took place in mid 2015 to convey surplus excavated spoil from Ferniehurst (south of Stow) to Falahill where it was incorporated in the landscaping of the vast quarry. This involved a six-week period of lorry movements along the A7 between the two locations. By June, the majority of the stations were complete and just awaited installation of the final fittings such as seats, shelters and ticket machines.

Over 2,200 people responded to ScotRail's recruitment campaign for drivers for the Borders Railway. In total, 64 drivers and 64 conductors trained for the new line. Of these 36 drivers and conductors were recruited locally. All underwent an intensive training schedule to prepare them for the launch of driver training runs on the line commencing in the summer of 2015.

Prior to the commencement of driver training, on 7 June 2015 'Border' Class 170 No 170414 was used for a proving run with the train stopping at each station to allow gap clearances between the train and the platform to be measured, seen taking place here at Tweedbank. *Iona Butlin*

Driver training commenced on 8 June 2015 using Class 158 No 158741 seen here north of Torwoodlee. *Iona Butlin*

The first 'passenger' train to travel the length of the line was Class 170 No 170414 which worked south on 7 June 2015 on a proving run stopping at every station to measure stepping distances between the platforms and the train. Driver training commenced the following day using Class 158 No 158741.

In connection with the start of driver training, Keith Brown visited the trainees at Tweedbank. On average, four return journeys were planned for each day between Tweedbank and Newcraighall. Training was completed by 28 August in readiness for the new service.

A significant milestone was reached on 14 June with the formal contract completion for BAM Nuttall, and the new railway was officially transferred to the ScotRail Alliance team – formed of Network Rail and Abellio. The final line-side construction works were undertaken during a four-day period from 16–19 July during which time driver training was halted. Work during these few days included installation of fencing, telecoms, minor earth works, drainage and lighting.

During July 2015, tickets went on sale for a series of what was to be sell-out steam services between Waverley and Tweedbank over a six-week period on Wednesdays, Thursdays and Sundays commencing on 10 September and using former LNER 'A4' No 60009 *Union of South Africa*, a class regularly seen on the former Waverley Route, giving people the chance to appreciate the new Borders Railway from the wonderful setting of a vintage steam train. It was also a fabulous opportunity to showcase Scotland's newest railway line, and in such a romantic style. ScotRail initiated the services on the grounds that there can be few railway journeys which match the outstanding scenery on this new route. Steam services running on the re-opened Borders Railway would really recapture the golden age of Scottish rail travel. The services also had strong support from VisitScotland who saw both the new line and the steam services as a fantastic opportunity for Scottish tourism.

To launch the new train services, individuals and organisations were invited to nominate worthy recipients for a 'Golden Ticket' so allowing them to travel on special trains on Saturday 5 September. Amongst the many initiatives surrounding the event, in the spirit of Roald Dahl's *Charlie and the Chocolate Factory*, Scottish Borders Council commissioned Cocoa Black, a local company, to produce a limited-edition chocolate bar supported by ScotRail. During the week 24-28 August 2015 every pupil in the 72 Primary and Secondary schools along the route each received a bar with one per school containing a lucky Golden Ticket for the special trains on 5 September.

During the summer of 2015 rumours circulated that a member of the Royal Family would be opening the new railway. All became clear on 3 August when it was announced that Her Majesty the Queen would officially open the railway on 9 September, the same date that she would become the longest serving monarch in British history.

Above: Prior to the opening of the railway, Class 170 No 170414 was used to take members of the local and national press on a run from Edinburgh Waverley to Tweedbank and back. Amongst the events laid on to promote the new line was the appearance at Tweedbank of the Braw Lad and riders from Galashiels Common Riding seen here at the station entrance. *Iona Butlin*

Middle: In connection with the opening of the Borders Railway, a number of trains ran the length of the railway carrying members of the public who had been nominated as worthy recipients of a Golden Ticket award for services to their community, or similar. Among them were Doug and Marian Smith and Jim and Helen Barnett from Greenlaw who are seen eagerly waiting to board the train at Tweedbank along with almost 200 others on 5 September 2015 *Iona Butlin*

Right: Crowds gather at Tweedbank station armed with their Golden Tickets. *Iona Butlin*

Immediately prior to the opening weekend, on 4 September ScotRail ran a press trip from Waverley to Tweedbank and back on the line using Class 170 No 170414 for members of local, national and railway press along with officials and local councillors.

The weekend of Saturday 5 and Sunday 6 September 2015 had to be experienced to appreciate the carnival atmosphere that pervaded the length of the line. From Waverley through to Tweedbank crowds gathered on the Saturday to witness the first trains to be filled by winners of the Golden Tickets.

Even the weather seemed to join in the celebrations as bright sunshine greeted these first passengers.

The following day found queues gathering at Tweedbank to catch the 08.45 service to Edinburgh, the first passenger paying train on the re-opened line. At the head of the queue were Andrew Whitworth from Harrogate and Miles Glendinning from Edinburgh who had been queuing since before 06.00!

The first public train on Sunday 6 September 2015 was the 08.45 Tweedbank–Edinburgh Waverley headed by refurbished Class 158 No 158701 with driver Stuart McLeod at the controls. *Iona Butlin*

At the head of the queue on the first morning were Andrew Whitworth from Harrogate and Miles Glendinning from Edinburgh who had been queuing since before 06.00! *Iona Butlin*

Throughout the Sunday, trains were filled to capacity as young and old alike either experienced travelling on the former Waverley Route for the first time, or relived past memories when they last travelled on the line.

On Wednesday 9 September the culmination of the re-opening reached its climax when Her Majesty the Queen, accompanied by the Duke of Edinburgh, First Minister Nicola Sturgeon and 150 invited guests travelled south from Waverley on a train hauled by former LNER 'A4' Pacific No 60009 *Union of South Africa* to open the line. Vast crowds lined the route as the train initially stopped at Newtongrange where a plaque was unveiled before the train continued to Tweedbank. Here staging had been erected to seat thousands who witnessed Her Majesty unveil a further plaque. The First Minister also made a speech in which she said:

'I want to start by acknowledging the milestone which makes this a historic day for many people far beyond the Scottish Borders. Her Majesty today becomes the longest serving monarch in Scottish and UK history.

'Throughout her reign – supported at all times by the Duke of Edinburgh – she has carried out her duties with dedication, wisdom and an exemplary sense of public service. As a result, Her Majesty is admired and held in affection across the Commonwealth and around the world. The reception she has received today, demonstrates that that admiration and affection is certainly felt here in Scotland.

'The very first public opening Her Majesty performed, as Princess Elizabeth, was in Scotland – at the Aberdeen Sailors' Home in 1944. Perhaps the proudest possession of the new Scottish Parliament is the mace she presented to us when we reconvened in 1999. Her Majesty has undertaken thousands of engagements across this nation including – last year – the opening of the Glasgow Commonwealth Games. And of course, her affection for Scotland was shared by Queen Victoria, whose memory she respects so much. In fact, when Queen Victoria became the longest-serving monarch, she was also in Scotland – staying at Balmoral.

'So it is fitting that Her Majesty has chosen to mark today's milestone here. And all of us are delighted to be able to share some of this day with her. By being here, she is adding a special touch to what is already a special day – for the Scottish Borders, for Midlothian, and for Scotland as a whole.

'I know that there will be some people here who have campaigned for a Borders rail link to be re-opened, virtually from the day it was closed. It has been a long time – 46 years – in coming. But today, I'm delighted that their persistence has seen a reward.'

One month after the opening, ScotRail announced that over 125,000 passengers had travelled on the line. In addition, 18 special steam trains had carried over 6,000 passengers between Edinburgh and Tweedbank on Wednesdays, Thursdays and Sundays.

Working hard up the grade from Tynehead to Falahill, former LNER Class A4 No 60009 *Union of South Africa* makes the hills at Cowbraehill echo to the sound of steam and the iconic chime whistle associated with the class as the train conveyed Her Majesty the Queen from Edinburgh Waverley to Tweedbank on Wednesday 9 September. The Royal party travelled in Pullman Car *Pegasus* seen behind the support coach. *Iona Butlin*

Overview of the Stations

Shawfair

On 18 July 2013 Midlothian Councillor Jim Bryant, cabinet member for economic development, joined with the Borders Railway project team in a ceremony at Shawfair station to launch the building of the station as major excavation works got underway.

Eskbank

Eskbank is one of the stations on the line to be relocated from its former site to one considered to be much more convenient for today's needs. In former days, Hardengreen Junction was an important location on the line south of Dalkeith and the previous Eskbank station, being the

Situated near the former Monktonhall Colliery, Shawfair is a new development on the outskirts of Edinburgh which over the next 25 years will see almost 4,000 new homes along with business opportunities. In addition to the station which is situated in the heart of the new development, the area will also have a new bus interchange, and paths and cycle networks provided by Midlothian Council. Situated on one of the dynamic passing loops, Shawfair, along with Stow, has two platforms serving up and down trains.

junction for the Peebles loop and to collieries in the Dalkeith area. An extensive array of sidings at the junction included a stabling point for locos employed as bankers to Falahill. Following closure the site was cleared and totally redeveloped including a large supermarket with extensive parking to the west of the line, while to the east is the Edinburgh College campus. Also nearby is the new Midlothian Community Hospital. Locating the new station in the midst of these developments, and linking it all by footpaths, was a logical development and makes the station here one of the most important in Midlothian.

Left: **A pair of Class 158 units Nos 158727 and 158701 stand at Eskbank on 10 September 2015.** *Iona Butlin*

Below: **Observed at Shawfair on 10 September 2015 Class 158 No 158718 departs with an Edinburgh-bound service.** *Iona Butlin*

Newtongrange

Another station to be relocated on the new line from its previous site, Newtongrange was once a thriving mining community. With mining long finished it is now home to the National Mining Museum Scotland. In connection to this, the new station is alongside the museum which is linked by a footpath to the station. Early indications are that the railway has been greatly beneficial to the museum and school parties make good use of the railway for their visits.

Gorebridge

Unlike other new stations, Gorebridge is at the same location as the previous station. New housing developments in the town benefit from the 30-minute journey to the centre of Edinburgh making the town popular with city commuters who seek a quieter life in the countryside.

Right: **Newtongrange station is situated alongside the National Mining Museum Scotland. On 26 August 2016 Class 158 No 158782 waits to depart for Edinburgh.** *Iona Butlin*

Below: **A pair of Class 170 units Nos 170414 and 170458 depart from Gorebridge for Tweedbank on 6 September 2015.** *Iona Butlin*

Stow

Stow is a small Border community with a population of just over 700 residents. Initial plans for the line did not include a station at Stow but pressure from the Campaign for Borders Rail resulted in the station being included at its former location alongside the new primary school. Another station on a dynamic loop with two platforms results in trains stopping at both platforms simultaneously as they pass. Unlike other stations, for much of the day Stow only has an hourly service, alternate trains not stopping here.

Galashiels

This large Border town previously had an extensive railway system with a large station, goods yard and engine shed. Today's station is a mere shadow of its predecessor being a single platform relocated north of the previous site, alongside Ladhope Vale and the new bus Interchange. Passenger numbers from the town are much greater than predicted and the town clearly benefits from the line with new housing developments reportedly selling fast as people take advantage of the commuter opportunities. Interestingly, the steam specials also stop at Galashiels on their way to and from Tweedbank.

Above: **Class 158 No 158704 departs north under the new footbridge on 23 September 2015.** *Iona Butlin*

Left: **Situated next to the Interchange building, Galashiels station is a shadow of its former self but is almost certainly far busier than its predecessor with a train to Edinburgh every 30 minutes. On 31 October 2015, Class 158 No 158735 waits to depart to Edinburgh.** *Iona Butlin*

Tweedbank

Scottish Borders Council leader David Parker joined with the BAM Construction team and representatives of Network Rail at Tweedbank on 23 July 2013 for a ceremony to start excavation works at the station site. At the time construction work commenced at Tweedbank, Hugh Wark, Project Director for the Borders Railway, said:

'The start of construction work at the site of Tweedbank station brings the railway into the heart of the Scottish Borders. It will provide modern facilities and ample park and ride space to enable train users from Selkirk, Melrose and Newton St Boswells, Hawick, and elsewhere in Scottish Borders to easily access the new line.'

The new station in the heart of the Scottish Borders is alongside the new town of Tweedbank which has grown up since the Waverley Route closed in 1969. Following pressure by the Campaign for Borders Rail, the station has a long island platform allowing charter trains to make use of the station without interrupting regular service trains. With extensive parking facilities and good bus links to Melrose and Galashiels, Tweedbank is the present terminus of the line, but one which many hope will only be temporary once the line goes on towards Hawick and possibly Carlisle.

Communication with the Public

In order to keep the public fully informed about the progress of the railway and the impact its construction would leave on peoples' lives, a series of public meetings commenced in November 2012 across Midlothian and the Scottish Borders. Residents had the opportunity to meet members of the team and discuss the detailed plans with over 1,200 attending the first 10 meetings at locations between Edinburgh and Galashiels.

A further round of drop-ins for the public followed in April 2013 to keep the public fully updated on developments especially as progress became increasingly evident throughout the route. Questions raised by members of the public included whether stations would have free parking, assurance being given that this would be the case.

Further drop-in sessions took place at the end of November and early December to keep the public informed of developments with the project now a year into the rebuild. Available at the meetings was a range of photographs and maps for members of the public to view.

Lying under the Eildon Hills, Tweedbank station has proved to be an outstanding success with passenger numbers way in excess of predicted figures. On a grey day and with the Eildon Hills in the background, Class 158 No 158738 waits to depart to Edinburgh on 23 September 2015. *Iona Butlin*

One of the regular meetings with the public included a drop-in evening at Stow Primary School on 11 June 2014 during the afternoon and evening, prior to work commencing on building the new station alongside the school. The Tweedbank Fair held on the first weekend of June 2014 had similar support by the Borders Railway Team who set up a stand to highlight the forthcoming railway to the local community.

One consequence of the closure of the Waverley Route in 1969 was that for over 40 years children grew up with no experience of railways and the related safety issues. Network Rail teamed up with the Scottish Youth Theatre (SYT) to present 24 rail safety workshops to children in 12 primary and secondary schools along the length of the new line during May and June 2013.

The following month, Transport Minister Keith Brown launched a dedicated British Transport Police team in July 2013 to patrol the Borders Railway Project. The team consisting of an inspector, a sergeant and several constables worked closely with Network Rail and BAM to look after the 30-mile site. Based at the site office in Newtongrange the team not only patrolled the railway but also attended community events.

As part of the building project, Borders Railway and the Scottish Community Safety Network made funds of £250 available each to 10 worthy local community projects in the summer of 2013. Amongst the recipients was Newtongrange Primary School which used the money to enhance their playground cycleway for cycling proficiency.

Twenty community groups along the length of the line shared a further £2,500 funding distributed in April 2014.

The Community Fund made its final payout of £6,000 in March 2015, bringing payouts totalling £15,000 to 70 local groups. Amongst the final recipients was a local dance group, a heritage centre and a junior football team.

Amongst other recipients of the final payout were Tweedbank Playgroups 'Choo-Choose to be safe' project which educated 2-5 year olds on the importance of rail safety. Stow Primary School used funds to put on a 'Past, Present & Future' project to celebrate the history of the railway in the Borders.

Veteran Campaigner

One name has become synonymous with the closure and re-opening of the railway, namely Madge Elliot from Hawick. Madge led the opposition to the closure of the railway in 1969 and along with David Steel (now Lord Steel) and the Earl of Dalkeith delivered a petition to Prime Minister Harold Wilson at 10 Downing Street on 18 December 1968. In 1999 Madge was a co-founder of the Campaign for Borders Rail, a

The only building at Tweedbank when the new station opened was the traincrew centre. In October 2015 pupils from Tweedbank Primary School ran a competition and named the building Eildon View.
Iona Butlin

Keith Brown and Madge Elliot stand alongside Freightliner Class 66 No 66528 following its naming at Edinburgh Waverley on 4 June 2015. *Iona Butlin*

Looking extremely proud, Madge Elliot holds her own memento nameplate at the naming ceremony. *Iona Butlin*

pressure group that pushed for the re-opening of the line and a restoration of passenger services to the Borders. To honour the work that Madge carried out over the years, Freightliner formally marked the occasion by naming one of its Class 66 locomotives, No 66528, *Madge Elliot MBE Borders Railway Opening 2015* in a ceremony at Edinburgh Waverley station on 4 June 2015. Madge along with family and friends was piped into the station and greeted by Keith Brown, Hugh Wark and Paul Smart (Freightliner MD) where she had the honour of unveiling the name plate. On the same day a giant artwork to celebrate the opening of the railway was unveiled at Waverley station.

Madge's elder son, Kim Elliot said:

'For as long as I can remember, the railway has been a passion for my parents, but for my mother in particular, and it's become a life-long interest for us all. We are delighted that, just days before trains start running on the railway once again, the project team has taken the opportunity to honour the role my mother played in re-establishing this link. It's a fitting tribute to her that the engine carrying her name has been used to build this railway and hopefully many more.'

In addition to the naming, Madge Elliot and her family had the privilege of being the 'first' passengers on the new Borders Railway when they were invited to travel from Tweedbank to Waverley on a driver training run on Sunday 26 July.

Process of Track Laying

Before track laying can take place, drains are installed to prevent the line from becoming waterlogged, an essential feature given the high rainfall experienced in the Scottish Borders. Following this, the ground is compacted to minimise later upward movement of soils into the ballast. A layer of bottom ballast is then laid on the formation and levelled to the correct depth. In total 130,000 tonnes of bottom ballast was required for the length of the line.

The line of the track is then accurately marked out on the ballast layer so that the sleepers can be laid out prior to rails being laid. Approximately 95,000 sleepers were required for the railway, using a modified excavator placing five at a time. Around 700 yards of sleepers could be placed on the trackbed each day. In preparation for the track laying, the sleepers were pre-fitted with Pandrol Fastclips.

A block of five sleepers held by an hydraulic clamp are lowered onto the ballast at Tweedbank station. Note the white guideline marked out on the ballast to aid accurate positioning of the sleepers prior to the track laying machine in the background moving round to lay the final rails. *Iona Butlin*

The rails were laid using a technique developed by BAM Rail in Holland, and required a work force of around 15 to lay the 118-yard lengths of track in pairs onto the sleepers, each pair of rails taking about 35 minutes to complete.

In all, 7,000 tonnes of rail were required for the new line and these were supplied by Tata Steel at Scunthorpe. Special rail-carrying wagons, five per train, carried 24 lengths of rail. Four rakes of wagons were used: one rake being loaded at Scunthorpe, two rakes transporting the rails between Scunthorpe and Millerhill Yard, and a final rake on site delivering the rails.

GB Railfreight provided the Class 66 locomotives used on site. Top-and-tailing the wagons onto the first dynamic loop, one loco running around the train so that both locomotives were at the rear and propelling the train forward to the track-laying machine where the track laying commenced.

The track laying machinery consisted of a number of units. The main roller unit was connected to the rail train and in turn was connected to a power unit. This was preceded by an auxiliary roller and winch unit. Separate was a mobile rail positioning unit on caterpillar tracks.

Observed at Shawfair on October 7 2014, the three-part unit is seen being propelled onto the first section of the Borders Railway with two rails drawn forward off the rail wagons waiting to be connected to the mobile unit. *Iona Butlin*

A worker moves along the sleepers ahead of the track machine laying rollers at regular intervals to guide the rails into place as they are moved forward. *Iona Butlin*

The track machine has been propelled to the end of the previously laid rails, and the roller unit draws the next two rails forward ready to be attached to the mobile caterpillar unit. *Iona Butlin*

Now the rails have been attached to the mobile unit which is drawing the rails forward over the sleepers, their position being aided by the mobile rollers. *Iona Butlin*

With the rails pulled clear of the track machine a small gap remains between the two ends. Winches are attached to the nearly laid rails and they are pulled back to the existing rails. *Iona Butlin*

With the two ends in place, they are clamped together prior to being welded at a later date. *Iona Butlin*

The mobile unit now lifts the rails to allow the rollers to be removed. *Iona Butlin*

Meanwhile, at the far end of the nearly laid rails the ends are cut between a pair of sleepers in preparation for the next pair of rails being laid. *Iona Butlin*

Robel clipping machines are attached to each rail and used to initially clip every fourth Pandrol Fastclip. *Iona Butlin*

Almost the end as the train works its way south through Galashiels station on 3 February 2015. Most aspects of the process can be seen in this view. *Iona Butlin*

End of the line at Tweedbank. *Iona Butlin*

Clearly proud of their achievements, the Dutch team have every reason to sing their own praises! Let us hope they will back in the near future to take the rails on to Hawick. *Iona Butlin*

Once the rails were in place, the sleepers needed stabilising using top ballast; 90,000 tonnes of which was required. This took place about a week later and involved a 30-wagon train top-and-tailed by Freightliner Class 66s. With the top ballast in place, the rail joints were welded together using a flash butt welding machine. The track could then be tamped and the rails stressed. Finally an automatic finishing machine was used to achieve the correct ballast profile.

Freightliner provided the motive power for the ballast trains. On 9 February 2015 Class 66 No 66601 heads a lengthy train north of Torwoodlee cutting. *Iona Butlin*

Observed near Bowland, Swietelsky Babcock Rail Tamper No DR73941 slowly makes its way south stabilising the track formation on 20 January 2015. *Iona Butlin*

Wildlife

One of the first signs of work on the new line was vegetation clearance on the trackbed. Over time trees had taken hold and now over 40 years old were well established. Viewed from the A7 which follows the line for considerable distances, piles of wood chips appeared on the trackbed as trees were removed and chipped. Prior to this taking place, detailed ecological studies were undertaken to evaluate each and every habitat associated with the line. When the original line was built by navvies back in the 19th century, wildlife conservation was an unknown concept, building going ahead with no regard to habitat protection or environmental impact. Reports from the mid 18th century reported that even otters were common in the Gala Water. Simple measures such as limiting vegetation clearance to outside the breeding season of birds was an essential conservation measure while water courses and aquatic species required a more pro-active approach with species such as lampreys requiring to be physically relocated. In other areas water courses were temporarily diverted to prevent pollution entering the water. Animals such as badgers, which are protected, needed special attention especially where they had constructed setts in embankments. Other species including barn owls and otters also required protection.

During the summer of 2013 over 70 juvenile lampreys were temporarily moved from the Gala Water to protect them during the nearby building works. Ecology experts identified a small group of Pipistrelle and Myotis (mouse eared) bats resident in Bowshank Tunnel. To protect the bats, special precautions were taken to safely remove them to bat boxes provided in nearby trees. The tunnel was then sealed to prevent the bats returning while work was undertaken on the tunnel structure.

In the spring of 2014, construction was at its height and the impact on breeding birds a major consideration. Every effort was made to protect species from covering structures with netting to providing exclusion zones around species like oystercatchers.

Andrew Mitchell, Project Environment Specialist for Network Rail, said:

'An essential part of the re-development of the Borders Railway is to ensure that we are protecting species that have been integral to the Midlothian and Scottish Borders environment for many years.

'Although it is inevitable that a project of this scale will require some de-vegetation and other disturbance to make way for the new line, we are committed to working with Scottish Natural Heritage and Scottish Environment Protection Agency in their regulatory capacity to make sure we work around important habitats and protected species or plants sensitively and, of course, appropriately.

'The Borders Railway project is also working to ensure any protected plant species are appropriately managed, one of which includes water crowfoot at various locations along the Gala Water.

'At this sensitive time of year our focus shifts from preventing nesting opportunities for birds towards identifying where nests may have been established and protecting them during the sensitive breeding period until the young have fledged.

'As part of our wider landscape and habitat commitments we are also identifying ways to enhance habitats and maximise the benefit of our longer term planting works for breeding birds.'

Iona Butlin

Iona Butlin

Tourism

As stated in the introduction, the Scottish Borders have a wealth of history, heritage, outstanding scenery, and ways of life that have remained unchanged over many years. When the Waverley Route closed in 1969, many tourist attractions felt the impact, having to rely on local buses and private cars to bring in visitors. Now, almost 50 years later, tourism has changed from the 1960s, and methods of promotion are very different from the past. The Internet alone has completely changed how people plan a day out or discover local attractions from abbeys to cafes, historic houses to restaurants. The re-opening of the railway was a tremendous boost to so many businesses and tourist attractions, and one backed by many who could see the opportunities the new line could bring especially in attracting some of the four million visitors that come to Edinburgh each year. Top amongst the many attractions, Sir Walter Scott exudes his presence from Waverley station, and the Scott Monument on Princes Street, to Abbotsford House, his former home, an easy walk or bus ride from Tweedbank station. A newly opened visitor centre at

Abbotsford tells the story of the world renowned writer, as well as providing a high quality restaurant and tea room. The house and gardens make for an equally pleasant visit.

It was after a series of Scott's novels that the Waverley Route was named, along with a number of NBR Class J (later LNER Classes D29 and D30) steam locomotives that worked the line which were named after characters in his novels. Some of these had extraordinary names including *'Dandie Dinmont'*, a farmer in *Guy Mannering*; *'Wandering Willie'*, a blind fiddler in *Red Gauntlet*; *'Jingling Geordie'*, a goldsmith in *The Fortunes of Nigel*; and *'Cuddie Headrigg',* a peasant in *Old Mortality*.

The date 15 August marks the writer's birthday and in 2015, just three weeks before the opening of the railway, two Dandie Dinmont Terriers, a breed of dog named and owned by Sir Walter Scott, travelled to Waverley station in his honour. Named after the former Dandie Dinmont in the novel *Guy Mannering*, the Dandie is the only dog breed believed named after a fictional character. Sir Walter Scott helped promote the popularity of the breed and it is thought every Dandie in the world can trace its pedigree back to a dog bred by Sir Walter Scott.

Situated alongside the A7 road as it enters Galashiels and over-looking the former station and yard, this plaque and locomotive were erected to commemorate the official opening of the Borders Railway on 9 September 2016. *Iona Butlin*

It was not only a Class 170 unit that was regaled in vinyls depicting the new railway. Two local buses received similar treatment and were a common sight in the Borders including the smaller of the two seen here at Tweedbank station. *Iona Butlin*

Mike Cantlay, Chairman of VisitScotland said:

'Sir Walter Scott's birth date is an appropriate landmark to celebrate three weeks to go until the Borders Railway opens up Scott country to the world. The Dandie Dinmont is such an iconic, rare breed, originating from the Scottish Borders, I would not be surprised if there was another rush to own one in the future!

'We are excited that we are moving ever closer to the launch of this magnificent new line and we are working with partners to ensure the tourism potential of our Borders Railway is fully realised both nationally and internationally, encouraging visitors to explore yet more of Scotland's beautiful urban and rural landscapes.'

Paul Keevil, Co-ordinator of the Dandie Dinmont – 200 years campaign, added:

'It is a very special year for the Dandie Dinmont Terrier in the Borders. We celebrated a 200th anniversary at Abbotsford in February and now we have the honour of supporting the countdown to the Borders Railway. We hope many people will discover the wonderful landscape and history of the Borders and, who knows, perhaps discover another of Scotland's hidden treasures – the Dandie Dinmont – as well!'

In this day and age, it is easy to forget that the original Edinburgh & Dalkeith Railway was opened to move coal from the Dalkeith area to Edinburgh. Over the years, coal remained a mainstay of freight on the line due to the insatiable appetite for the fuel in the capital and beyond. Today the Lothian coalfields are history, so much so that the National Mining Museum Scotland is now based at the former Lady Victoria Colliery, Newtongrange. Linked to the newly relocated Newtongrange station, the museum is attracting numerous visitors aided by the frequent services serving the station.

Historically it was the novels of Sir Walter Scott that helped publicise the original Waverley Route. Today, the *Da Vinci Code* novel by Dan Brown has promoted Rosslyn Chapel – just a short bus ride from Eskbank station, it is another tourist location to benefit from the re-opening of the line. Whether trains will be named after Dan Brown novels and associated characters as per the Waverley novels remains to be seen!

A train ride of less than 30 minutes can bring you from the centre of Edinburgh to the tranquillity of Gore Glen Woodland Park or Vogrie Country Park. Beyond Gorebridge the railway climbs into the Southern Upland Hills offering outstanding views and walking and cycling for those leaving the train at Stow and Galashiels.

Tweedbank will hopefully be a temporary terminus for the railway with much pressure being placed towards re-opening the line through Melrose, St Boswells and on to Hawick. In the meantime, visitors for the many attractions on offer at Melrose must make the short journey from Tweedbank either by bus or on foot. Amongst the sites at Melrose is the world renowned Melrose Abbey, founded by King David I in 1136 and famed as the burial place of Robert the Bruce's heart.

The First Year

Even before the rails had been laid at Tweedbank, thoughts and talk turned to extending the line to Hawick and even Carlisle. Championed by the Campaign for Borders Rail, lobbying of local and national government has constantly promoted the benefits to the Borders in extending the line south.

Scepticism from some groups throughout the building of the line to the point of some individuals voicing the concept that the project would be a total disaster culminating in the closing of the line. These views were rapidly buried on the opening of the line in September 2015 as passengers flocked to the stations. Equally, comments that it would be a short-lived revival, falling off as time progressed, were also proved

There is virtually no chance that Selkirk will ever again see trains arrive from Galashiels as in the past but this did not stop the town celebrating the re-opening including the creation of a knitted train attached to railings near the site of the long closed Selkirk station.
Iona Butlin

In former days, teams of platelayers patrolled the route on a daily basis checking that all was well with the trackwork. That approach has long gone, replaced today by highly sophisticated test trains that can monitor all aspects of the line so ensuring the safety of passengers and staff alike. These trains run regularly over the network including the Borders Railway. To avoid interfering with the intense daytime services, Tweedbank is visited at night after the passenger services cease. On 12 February 2016, Class 37 No 37057 and DBSO No 9703 top-and-tailed test vehicles Nos 72639, 977974 and 6263 in a snow storm at Tweedbank. *Iona Butlin*

wrong when overall usage of the line almost reached 700,000 in the first six months, 22% above prediction. Given that this is not a time of the year associated normally with tourism, it indicates that it is resident Borderers making most use of the new service.

Actual passenger figures for individual stations against projected numbers

Station	Projected	Actual
Tweedbank	18,978	183,918
Galashiels	20,567	104,593
Stow	5,129	24,365
Gorebridge	79,014	39,400
Newtongrange	46,449	50,480
Eskbank	114,568	65,672
Shawfair	54,298	9,398
Brunstane & Newcraighall	865	11,344
Edinburgh Waverley	228,156	205,203

These figures are open to various interpretations. Particularly noticeable is the greatly increased numbers travelling from Tweedbank, Galashiels and Stow above predicted figures, being more than 600%. Equally, less seem to be travelling from stations near Edinburgh. The most likely cause of the latter is the fact that house building has a long way to go at sites especially around Shawfair where the first 120 homes from a total of 4,000 are due to be ready by the winter of 2016/17, and the projected numbers were more akin to those to be expected in the future.

The validity of numbers carried can also be questioned due to overcrowding on the two-car Class 158s preventing conductors being able to check or sell tickets to all customers, free travel being all too possible if local social media is to be believed.

The success of the railway quickly had a knock-on effect with global IT company CGI announcing in early 2016 that it was to locate a digital centre of excellence in the Scottish Borders with the potential to create up to 200 new jobs.

In May 2016 Phil Verster, managing director of the ScotRail Alliance, said:

> *'It's clear that the success of the line has been a catalyst for other communities to champion their own rail links and we are working closely with partners to encourage and support economic growth across Scotland.*
>
> *'We have recently appointed a Borders Railway Programme Executive who is already working closely with the Blueprint Partnership to ensure the lasting legacy of the new line by encouraging and supporting economic growth throughout the regions the railway touches.'*

The Blueprint vision sees the Borders Railway acting as a catalyst to stimulate economic growth. An inward investment prospectus has been published promoting site-specific developments in housing, commercial and leisure sectors. These create major opportunities for existing and new businesses to take advantage of growing markets and new connectivity to and from Edinburgh city centre. There are also inward investment incentives through the new assisted area location in the railway corridor. Supporting the Blueprint, the Scottish Government has made a commitment to invest £10 million. An additional 57,000 jobs are forecast for Edinburgh City Region and 37,200 jobs forecast to be created in the Borders Railway area by 2030.

Throughout 2016 passenger numbers continued above expectation. Unfortunately, the railway was also hit by a number of serious problems in the summer months that had an adverse effect on all aspects of the railway. Signalling problems, lack of available units and staff shortages combined to see a fall in punctuality to 28.4% with some 70 services being cancelled over a 10-day period. ScotRail admitted that the situation was totally unacceptable especially with the problems associated with the Class 158 units which suffered radiator problems on the steep climb to Falahill. A replacement radiator programme was underway by late 2016 to rectify the problem.

Steam trains

One of the highlights of the new railway has been the steam train excursions run during the first two years. When Her Majesty the Queen travelled from Waverley to Tweedbank on 9 September 2015 behind former LNER 'A4' No 60009 *Union of South Africa* to officially open the line, it immediately became apparent that the return of steam to the Borders Railway would be an immense attraction. This was proved true in the following weeks when trains ran on Wednesdays, Thursdays and Sundays. Unfortunately there was a downside on Wednesdays and Thursdays as service trains had to be cancelled to facilitate pathing of the specials. With the steam locomotive at the south end of the train most photographers headed for locations north of Falahill where the train would be working hard and hopefully producing plenty of smoke and steam.

On 8 October 2015 the 'A4' *Union of South Africa* **bursts under the bridge at Fushiebridge as it heads south climbing towards Borthwick Bank and Falahill.** *Ashley Butlin*

Union of South Africa heads south from Bowshank Tunnel on 29 September 2015. *Iona Butlin*

All the services during 2015 were handled by No 60009. However, on 13 September newly built 'A1' No 60163 *Tornado* substituted for the 'A4' and is viewed climbing Borthwick Bank. *Steven Crozier*

The return to steam of former LNER 'A3' No 60103 *Flying Scotsman* was greeted with unacceptable behaviour around the country. Travelling north on the East Coast Main line, so-called enthusiasts brought service trains to a halt as they trespassed on the lines to see and photograph the engine. A planned trip on the Borders Railway for 15 May 2016 was initially cancelled for fear of a similar situation occurring. At the last minute, following considerable pressure, the train was re-instated and the iconic loco made a return to the line. Enormous crowds greeted the train and on the whole were well behaved, the only real problem was at Bowland on the A7 where motorists blocked the road due to inconsiderate or last minute parking bringing traffic to a standstill. Viewed heading down the grade towards Stow the train made a fine sight. As with all steam services on the line, a diesel is provided on the rear to power the train back but also insurance should the steam loco suffer a failure. On this date, Class 47 No 47580 was provided. *Iona Butlin*

Opposite top: Later the Pacific is simmering at Tweedbank as it waits for the special to head back to Edinburgh. *Iona Butlin*

Bottom: Following the success of the 2015 services, expectations for 2016 were high especially in the hope that there would be a change of locomotive. Initially plans were to share the service between 'A4' *Union of South Africa* and former LMS 4-6-0 No 46100 *Royal Scot*. In the event *Union of South Africa* was unavailable, requiring maintenance, so *Royal Scot* was used throughout August and September. A further change saw trains limited to Sundays only with two trips, one in the morning and one in the evening. On 28 August *Royal Scot* climbs towards Tynehead on the morning run to Tweedbank. *Iona Butlin*

All the steam trains had a diesel attached to the rear of the train, the diesel pulling the train back to Edinburgh. On 18 October 2015 Class 67 No 67026 waits at Tweedbank prior to heading north. *Iona Butlin*

Opposite top: On 7 August 2016 *Royal Scot* is seen near Bowland heading south with the morning service. *Iona Butlin*

Bottom: Until 9 October 2016, all steam trains ran with the locomotive at the front heading towards Tweedbank. However, a Scottish Railway Preservation Society (SRPS) tour on 9 October saw the train run from Edinburgh to Tweedbank hauled by a West Coast Railway's Class 37 with former LMS 'Black Five' No 45407 on the rear. From Tweedbank the 'Black Five' hauled the charter back to Edinburgh, across the Forth Bridge, around Fife and back across the Bridge and south to Tweedbank before the Class 37 took the train back north. On the outward journey, the 'Black Five' works hard up the gradient towards Heriot, the first steam locomotive to do so since the mid sixties. *Iona Butlin*

Diesel Railtours

A number of diesel-hauled railtours have reached Tweedbank since it opened including an SRPS tour from Tweedbank to the Kyle of Lochalsh and back on 7 May 2016, top-and-tailed by West Coast Railway Class 47 Nos 47826 and 47832. Arriving back in the early hours of Sunday 8 May, it remained at the station until later in the morning when it ran empty carriage stock (ecs) back to Edinburgh. *Iona Butlin*

A further tour on 18 June 2016 saw 'Deltic' Class 55 No 55009 *Alycidon* venture to Tweedbank from York assisted by Class 67 No 67022 on the rear. It is seen heading south out of Galashiels en-route to Tweedbank. This was the second time the locomotive had visited the new line, having previously headed a tour to the Borders on 9 April. *Iona Butlin*

Onward to Hawick?

Reinstating the line from Tweedbank through to Hawick is not impossible but will present a number of challenges. The policy of the new railway is to avoid level crossings, replacing previous ones with bridges. Tweedbank station car park is accessed by a flat crossing beyond the platform end. This will require a new entrance to the car park as will a number of minor roads in Tweedbank Industrial Estate.

Beyond Tweedbank further earthworks will be required to reinstate the line through to nearby Melrose. While the original trackbed is in place for much of the route, changes to the road system with the building of the A6091 Melrose bypass has encroached on parts of the trackbed in a number of places through to its junction with the A68 road. Realigning either the road and/or trackbed would seem quite feasible, connected with new bridges at the A68 junction.

Turning south, the line re-crossed the A68 road and entered Newtown St Boswells. Part of the trackbed remains but has been built over near the former station. Here the station was built on a bridge which has been removed leaving a 'gap' which will require to be replaced. As has been shown with the building of the new stations on the Borders Railway, much less space is required for a station than in the past. The south end of the former St Boswells station is an unadopted car park with adequate room for the building of a single platform. Centrally located in the town, it would be ideally suited for the nearby Scottish Borders Council Headquarters.

The trackbed is clearly defined as the railway leaves St Boswells although it has been breached in a number of locations. Moving south the first station out of St Boswells was Charlesfield, located on an overbridge and an area now abounding with wildlife. Passing through Belses will present a number of problems as the road bridges either side of the former station have been removed whilst the station is a private residence. No such problems should exist at Hassendean even though the station is also a private residence and the site much developed for holiday accommodation. Even the footbridge has been restored to its former glory. Tom Pyemont, the present owner of the site, is philosophical about the return of the railway. A keen supporter of the return of trains, he knows he and his family will need to move when this happens and although he will lose his home, he will not lose the many happy memories he has from living here. From here it is only a few miles through open countryside before the line reaches Hawick. Development in the Burnfoot area has severed the route in a number of places although none is too serious. Where a potential new station could be located is interesting and most likely just short of the previous station site now occupied by the town's leisure centre.

The up platform and station building at Melrose remain very much the same as they had been during operational days. However, the trackbed and down side of the station were swept away when the Melrose bypass was built. Reinstating the railway to Hawick will find this section a serious difficulty as much of the trackbed lies under the new road. *Iona Butlin*

South of the former Kelso Junction, new roadworks at the junction of the A6091 and A68 have cut through the trackbed twice in a matter of several hundred yards that will require considerable engineering works should the former route be followed in the future. Looking northwest, the A6091 Melrose Road passes from left to right, while the main A68 road is behind the photographer. *Iona Butlin*

A view today at St Boswells shows the shed is extant and in use by a local vehicle hire firm. It was being renovated in August 2016. The bay platform remains in place although covered in trees and the route south of the former Waverley Route was clearly defined and accessible on a footpath. *Iona Butlin*

Part of the station site to the south of the main buildings at St Boswells is now an unadopted car park and would make an ideal location for a new station built to the same style as others on the new Borders Railway. In this view the former bay platform used by Kelso trains is rapidly being overtaken by vegetation while the wall of the shed building is to the left. Newtown St Boswells is another Border town that should attract tourists if the line re-opens, due to the presence of nearby Dryburgh Abbey. *Iona Butlin*

A small station/halt was built here at Charlesfield in August 1942 to serve the nearby ammunitions factory. Today, the trackbed is used by a local farmer who has opened up an access track from the road; surrounded on both sides by trees and bushes, the area is a thriving habitat for flowers, birds and insects. Looking at the location it is difficult to imagine it as a newly re-opened line in the hopefully near future. *Iona Butlin*

Hassendean is another station to survive as a private residence, being converted in the 1980s by architect Tom Pyemont. The main station building has been extended and is the family residence, while the waiting room on the down platform is the office of Mr Pyemont's business. During 2016, he completed the restoration of the original footbridge to a high standard and it is visible from a number of locations around the area. Interestingly, although the site has become a wonderful home for Tom and his wife, along with the guests who stay in the converted goods shed, he is a keen enthusiast to see the line restored to Hawick even though it will be the end of his home as it is now. *Iona Butlin (both)*

Looking across Hawick along the former Waverley Route: the station was in the distance where the Leisure Centre is now located. In the foreground, the long embankment has been removed allowing the new link road to be built. *Iona Butlin*

While the arrival of the railway to Hawick would undoubtedly bring much needed visitors to the town, there are those local shop-keepers who worry that it could just as easily take customers away to Edinburgh for Princes Street and the Fort Kinnaird shopping complex alongside Newcraighall station.

Journey on the Borders Railway

Arriving at Tweedbank station mid-morning, the first problem is finding a space in the very busy car park. Although 235 places are available, only a few at the far end were vacant. Tweedbank station consists of an island platform long enough to hold a full-length charter train. Facilities initially were basic – a waiting shelter and ticket machine. However, in January 2017 a refreshment booth and toilet block were opened, both having been eagerly awaited and needed. Our train, the 11.28 to Edinburgh consists of the ubiquitous Class 158 two-car unit, is waiting and a reasonable number of passengers are already aboard. Departure is on time and in a matter of moments we are clearing the end of the platform and heading towards the Redbridge Viaduct spanning the River Tweed. Being single track, on the left there is sufficient space to retain a footpath/cycle way across the bridge linking Tweedbank with Galashiels.

Entering the outskirts of the town, on the left can be seen the town's rugby pitch and the former route of the branch to Selkirk. In the past, a string of mills lay alongside the railway and the Gala Water. Today the mills have gone and the area is an industrial estate. Our line climbs as we come alongside Currie Road and cross it on a new bridge. The large area that was Galashiels goods yard, engine shed and station has been turned over to the proverbial supermarket and retail shopping units. Passing these, the new line follows a route to the extreme northeast of the site and we slow as we come under the new Station Brae Bridge and enter the new station – a single platform alongside Ladhope Vale and the new Transport Interchange. Galashiels lacks station parking facilities but the new Interchange brings all buses to the station and is proving popular.

A good number of passengers join our train and following a brief stop we continue on our journey. To the right the line is bounded by a very high retaining brick wall. Passing under the A7 road we are again alongside the Gala Water and an area once home to further mills on both sides of the line. Retail units now dominate the area.

Galashiels was served by lines both direct from Edinburgh and via the Peebles loop which merged with the main line at Kilnknowe Junction. The bridge on our left with an extra arch shows evidence of the Peebles line prior to it diverging at the junction. Our line turns north and we soon pass through the short Torwoodlee Tunnel and enter the deep Torwoodlee cutting bounded on either side by a golf course.

The line opens up as we head north alongside the Gala Water with hills on both sides. Very shortly we are on one of the three dynamic passing loops and enter Bowshank Tunnel. To our right we are followed by the A7 road with its steady procession of vehicles. Shortly we begin to slow as we arrive at Stow, a location that was not initially planned to have a station. This decision was reversed following pressure from the Campaign for Borders Rail. Outside of peak travel times, alternate trains stop at the station. As we enter the station, to our left are new houses while to the right is Stow Primary School, and beyond the village. Stow, along with Shawfair, are the only stations with two platforms built on a dynamic passing loop and here we pass a southbound service en-route to Tweedbank.

North of Stow the line passes through spectacular Border countryside. For the wildlife enthusiasts there is plenty to see depending on the time of year. Numerous breeding oystercatchers can be seen alongside the water in the spring and early summer while buzzards can be seen at any time. The keen eyed may be fortunate to see deer and hares, both of which frequent these valleys. In the past both Fountainhall and Heriot had stations but not on the new line. In addition, both were linked to the A7 by level crossings but these have been replaced by new overbridges. Just south of Fountainhall the route of the former Lauder branch can be seen on the right.

The speed of our train is clearly decreasing, not because of a further station stop but due to the steep climb to Falahill which is reached beyond Heriot. A large bridge carries the A7 over the line at this point. On our left are the cottages of Falahill while on the opposite side, the open hillside belies the fact that this was a large quarry opened up during construction of the line but now landscaped and returned to farmland. You may be fortunate to just catch sight on your right of the lineside post indicating we have reached the summit and will now be heading downhill all the way to Edinburgh. Our route is circuitous due to the need for the original Waverley Route taking the easiest route possible to take the line over Falahill. At Falahill the line diverts away from the A7 which was able to follow a more direct route north. Our train soon enters a deep cutting at Tynehead, the possibility of this being a tunnel was initially considered but abandoned as cuttings are easier to construct and cheaper to maintain. Tynehead is also the southern end of a further passing loop. Considerable earthworks were required north of here as the line climbed Borthwick Bank.

Built near the extensive Fort Kinnaird shopping centre, Newcraighall opened on 3 June 2002. Equipped with a large Park and Ride car park, the single-platform station was built near the site of the second Niddrie station. Until the re-opening of the Borders Railway, Newcraighall was the terminus for trains to Edinburgh and Fife. On 26 August 2016, Class 158 No 158782 departs for Edinburgh. *Iona Butlin*

Many changes have taken place since the closure of the Waverley Route in 1969. North of Gorebridge lies Gore Glen Woodland Park. Lying off the A7, the park offers walkers an opportunity to access woodland areas through which runs the railway. Class 158 No 158869 heads south through the park on 15 September 2016. *Iona Butlin*

Class 158 No 158735 enters the dynamic loop on the approach to Fushiebridge while Class 170 No 170457 waits to continue north on 15 October 2015. The town of Gorebridge is in the distance.
Iona Butlin

Class 158 No 158718 descends Borthwick Bank on 15 September 2016. Borthwick Castle is out of view to the right of the picture.
Iona Butlin

Two castles are passed at this point: first on our right is Crichton Castle followed soon after on the left by Borthwick Castle. We continue our circuitous route north around the hills passing the site of Fushiebridge station, closed back in 1943, where we are briefly held at the end of the loop to allow a further southbound service to pass, until we approach the outskirts of Gorebridge, heralded by new housing development on our right. Built on a curve on the side of the hill, Gorebridge station is another with a single platform serving all trains and along with Stow, built new on the site of the former station. Continuing north we enter the wooded area of Gore Glen Woodland Park, popular with walkers.

Historically, this was a mining area; the original reason for the building of the railway was to transport coal to Edinburgh. On the right as we slow for Newtongrange station we pass the site of Lady Victoria Colliery, now home to the National Mining Museum Scotland. The majority of the land covered by the former railway sidings associated with the pit is now the Lady Victoria industrial complex housing a variety of businesses. The open countryside and hills of the Borders are now well behind us but to our left we catch glimpses of the Pentland Hills to the south of the city. After Newtongrange station we soon cross the impressive Lothianbridge Viaduct although it is easy not to realise its location from the train. Beyond this our line again crosses the A7 at Hardengreen Roundabout and enters Eskbank station. This area has changed out of all recognition since the Waverley Route closed back in 1969. New roads and redevelopment

Heading north through the Plumtree Brae area of Galashiels is a pair of Class 170 units led by No 170432 on a Sunday service on 14 August 2016. It is usually only on a Sunday when spare stock is available that the Class 170s work on the line. *Iona Butlin*

have obliterated all signs of the once extensive Hardengreen Junction where the line to Peebles diverged to our left. On the right, colliery lines converged on the array of sidings from where coal was transported away both north and south. Today a glimpse of a large Tesco supermarket may be had on the left while to the right the Midlothian campus of Edinburgh College is well served by the new station.

Leaving the new station we soon pass through a cutting and can see the platforms of the previous station which surprisingly were not removed when the line was rebuilt. Crossing the River North Esk the line soon takes a deviation away from the former Waverley Route. Passing under the City Bypass we enter the area of Shawfair. At present this is very much a brown field site but the coming years will see around 4,000 homes being built in the area. Just before passing under the City Bypass we entered the third passing loop which runs though Shawfair station to just short of where the line rejoins its former route at the top end of Millerhill Yard. Here we slow to stop at Newcraighall station which is ideally situated for

the nearby Fort Kinnaird shopping centre. Opened in 2002 Newcraighall was, and still is, a designated Park and Ride station for Edinburgh and we see that the large car park is well patronised. A short ride brings us to Brunstane. 'The Range' retail outlet adjoins the station on our left while a further campus of Edinburgh College is to the right.

From Brunstane we join the main line coming in on our right from Berwick-upon-Tweed and gradually make our way past the large Craigentinny carriage sheds on our left. These service the many main line trains at Edinburgh. To the left lies the great volcanic outcrop of Holyrood Park. Passing through Calton Hill Tunnel we arrive at Edinburgh Waverley station, our journey taking a fraction under the hour.

On arrival at Waverley we are greeted by the news that Transport Scotland has appointed Jacobs UK Ltd to investigate the possibility of extending the Borders Railway from Tweedbank to Carlisle, with their findings due by November 2017. The prospect of trains once again climbing to Whitrope Summit becomes a step nearer.

Overleaf: **North of Stow, the railway runs through beautiful countryside alongside the Gala Water. On 15 September 2016 Class 158 No 158871 heads south on a Tweedbank service.** *Iona Butlin*

Above: Class 158 No 158729 and a second unidentified unit head north out of the dynamic loop north of Stow station on 15 October 2015. *Iona Butlin*

North of the present station, the former Newtongrange station was a late addition being opened on 1 August 1908. Viewed from a new footbridge linking Station Road with Old Star Road, nothing remains of the former station site and only the street name gives a clue as to its location. Observed on 26 August 2016, Class 158 No 158707 slows for the new station as it rounds the bend on a southbound service for Tweedbank. *Iona Butlin*

Index